Seriously Good!

GLUTEN-FREE
BAKING

Seriously Good!
GLUTEN-FREE
BAKING

PHIL VICKERY

In association with

Photography by Tara Fisher

Kyle Books

This edition reprinted in 2011 by
Kyle Books
23 Howland Street, London W1T 4AY
general.enquiries@kylebooks.com
www.kylebooks.com

10 9 8 7 6 5 4 3

ISBN 978 1 85626 923 0

First published in Great Britain in 2010 by Kyle Cathie Ltd.

Project editor: Jenny Wheatley
Photographer: Tara Fisher
Designer: Jacqui Caulton
Food stylist: Annie Rigg
Props stylist: Wei Tang
Copy editor: Jane Bamforth
Editorial assistant: Elanor Clarke
Production: Gemma John

A Cataloguing In Publication record for this title is available
from the British Library.

Printed in China by C&C Offset Printing Co.,Ltd.

CONTENTS

FOREWORD

When I decided to write *Seriously Good! Gluten-Free Cooking* a couple of years ago, it was after I'd started a gluten-free Christmas pudding company. The response to the puddings was so huge that I wanted to find out more about gluten-free diets. While researching, it quickly became apparent that coeliac disease is a worldwide condition. So, the idea to write a book dedicated to gluten-free cooking seemed like the obvious route to take.

People from all over the world have sent me e-mails and letters in response to the book. From mums who couldn't find a gluten-free birthday cake recipe for their kids, to a lady in her 90s, finally being able to eat 'normal food' after 35 years with the condition – it's been a real eye-opener for me.

In the first book I covered all areas of cooking with a section on desserts and baking. While the feedback has been incredible, the overwhelming themes were requests for gluten-free Yorkshire puddings, birthday cakes, Christmas cake, Welsh cakes, sponges, cupcakes and of course bread!

So this book includes all of the above, plus new recipes for pastry, traybakes, muffins, biscuits and celebration cakes. Also look out for some slightly unusual recipes: Tangy Beetroot and Blackcurrant Muffins, Sweet Courgette and Saffron Butterfly Cakes, and Sweet Potato Thins all work really well and certainly take gluten-free baking a step further.

It has taken me about a year to write this book, partly due to me writing slowly, but also due to the fact that it takes an incredible amount of time to cook and perfect each recipe. Sometimes a new idea works first time (great, but it didn't happen very often!); mostly, though, it has taken up to three, four, five, six or even seven times to get it right! There have been many technical and scientific challenges to overcome to get the very best results each time, and I enlisted the help of my good friend, food scientist Bea Harling, to keep me on the straight and narrow. Her knowledge has been invaluable.

The final result is 70 recipes that I am very happy with. Some are far better, in my view, than conventional similar products, like the Vanilla Cupcakes for example. When it comes to bread there will always be the inevitable comparison to regular bread; sadly you will never mimic it perfectly without many additives and chemicals, something that I try to steer clear of. But I'm really pleased with the recipes in the Bread chapter and urge you to have a go – whether it's foccacia, savoury scones or teabread you'll discover that baking gluten-free bread truly can be rewarding.

I hope this book helps you in two ways: one, it inspires you to get in the kitchen so you can discover how delicious gluten-free baking can be! And also that it helps to highlight coeliac disease so that living on a gluten-free diet becomes easier in the future.

And finally don't forget...
People on a gluten-free diet can enjoy really delicious, flavourful food. In fact, a gluten-free diet not only offers the chance to improve the quality of the food you eat by cooking with fresh, unprocessed ingredients, but also helps to introduce your tastebuds to new flavour combinations. The recipes in this book are all about expanding your gluten-free diet – giving you food to enjoy, food that is nutritious and food that will make you feel... *Seriously Good!*

INTRODUCTION TO COELIAC DISEASE

If you have recently been diagnosed with coeliac disease, don't panic – here are answers to the most commonly asked questions, along with advice on what to eat and what to avoid.

What is coeliac disease?

Coeliac (pronounced seeliac) disease is often misunderstood. It is frequently regarded as an allergy or simple food intolerance, but it is actually a lifelong auto-immune disease affecting the gut and other parts of the body. The body's immune system reacts to the gluten found in food, making the body attack itself when gluten is eaten. Gluten is a protein found in wheat, barley and rye, and some people are also affected by oats. Gluten is a collective name for the type of protein found in these cereals. It is what gives bread its elasticity and cakes their spring.

People with coeliac disease are sensitive to gluten when it is eaten. The small intestine is lined with small, finger-like projections called villi. These play a crucial role in digestion, as they increase the surface area of the small intestine and allow essential nutrients to be absorbed into the bloodstream. However, for people with coeliac disease, when gluten comes into contact with the villi, it triggers a response by the immune system which attacks the villi as if it were a 'foreign' substance. The villi very quickly become damaged and inflamed and therefore incapable of extracting key nutrients from the food we eat. This results in a range of different problems with varying severity.

What are the symptoms?

There are a variety of gastrointestinal symptoms such as cramps, bloating, flatulence and diarrhoea. It is quite common for these to be confused with irritable bowel syndrome (IBS) and only later to be identified as coeliac disease.

TYPICAL SYMPTOMS OF COELIAC DISEASE

The symptoms vary in terms of severity. Most stem from the malabsorption of nutrients, and include diarrhoea, fatigue and iron deficiency, but there is a range of other symptoms, such as:

- Bloating
- Abdominal pains
- Nausea
- Tiredness
- Headaches
- Weight loss (but not in all cases)

- Mouth ulcers
- Hair loss
- Skin rash
- Defective tooth enamel
- Problems with fertility
- Recurrent miscarriages

Diarrhoea is a common symptom. Yet it is important to note that sufferers can present many and varied symptoms: some may have a normal bowel habit or even tend towards constipation, children may not gain weight or grow properly, while adults may find they lose weight. Malabsorption may also leave people tired and weak, due to anaemia caused by iron deficiency.

In fact, rather than suffering from bowel problems, many people with coeliac disease approach their doctor because of extreme tiredness (due to chronic, poor iron absorption) and psychological problems such as depression. There can also be a malabsorption of calcium, resulting in low bone density and sometimes even fractures (as a result of osteoporosis). Bone and muscle pain can also be a problem. Ulcers in the mouth or a blistering, itchy skin rash, mostly on the elbows and knees (called dermatitis herpetiformis), are also symptoms of coeliac disease.

Undiagnosed coeliac disease can result in infertility in both men and women and there is also an increased risk of miscarriage.

How do I get diagnosed?

First, if you suspect you may have coeliac disease, don't worry! Just remember, it is entirely manageable with a controlled diet. In fact, if you are one of the many undiagnosed people with coeliac disease you'll probably be pleased to find out that you really do have a condition and, better yet, that there is a course of action to make you well again.

There is a clear procedure for diagnosing coeliac disease. The first thing to do is talk through your symptoms with your GP, as they can perform a simple blood test. This test looks for antibodies which your body produces in response to gluten. It is important to follow your normal diet leading up to the test, as you need to have the antibodies in your blood for a test to work, and these will only be there if you have been eating gluten. It is quite common for people to go undiagnosed if they have followed a gluten-free diet for days or weeks, as the immune system will be producing fewer antibodies. This will give a false, negative result to the test. To get an accurate result it is important to consume food that contains gluten in at least one meal a day, for a minimum of six weeks, before a blood test.

If the test is positive, it is recommended that people then have an intestinal biopsy, which examines the appearance of the villi in the small intestine, under a microscope, to check for damage. This will confirm the diagnosis, which you need before you start on a lifelong gluten-free diet. Again, the biopsy of the small intestine must be done whilst you're following a gluten-based diet. If you are already following a gluten-free diet when you have your biopsy, it might show a completely normal intestinal lining or you may have an inconclusive result.

What is the treatment?

Coeliac disease is treated with a gluten-free diet, so wheat, barley, rye and any derived ingredients must all be avoided. The most obvious sources of gluten in the diet are pastas, cereals, breads, flours, pizza bases, pastry, cakes and biscuits. Oats can often be contaminated with other grains, and although most people are able to tolerate uncontaminated oats without a problem, some people with coeliac disease may be sensitive and should avoid them. Uncontaminated oats are available but should be tried under supervision of your healthcare team.

Following a strict gluten-free diet allows the intestines to heal and the alleviation of symptoms in most cases. Depending on how early on the gluten-free diet is started, it can also eliminate the increased risk of osteoporosis and cancer of the small bowel.

What can I eat?

There are plenty of foods that are naturally gluten-free and should be included in your diet. In particular, carbohydrate-rich foods such as potatoes, rice and maize do not contain gluten. All fresh meat, poultry and fish, all fresh fruit and vegetables, fresh herbs, individual spices, dried pulses, rice noodles, potatoes, plain nuts, eggs, dairy products, sugar, honey, oils and vinegars, vanilla essence and extract and fresh and dried yeast are suitable. In fact, the gluten-free diet has the potential to be one of the healthiest diets around because of the increased emphasis placed upon eating fresh, natural and unprocessed food. If undiagnosed coeliac disease has resulted in the poor absorption of vitamins and minerals, a gluten-free diet should soon restore these to healthy levels and lead to a feeling of health and wellbeing.

More and more manufacturers are producing gluten-free substitute foods, such as gluten-free bread, crackers and pasta, some of which can be just as good as their gluten-containing equivalents. Coeliac UK publishes a Food and Drink Directory annually which is a list of nearly 10,000 gluten-free products.

GLUTEN-FREE FOODS

- All fresh meat and fish
- All fresh fruit and vegetables
- Fresh herbs and individual spices
- Polenta (ground cornmeal or maize)
- Dried peas, lentils, pulses and beans
- Rice and wild rice
- Rice bran
- Rice noodles
- Plain nuts and seeds
- Eggs
- Dairy products – milk, cream, natural yogurt, cheese
- Soya and plain tofu
- Sugar
- Honey
- Golden syrup
- Maple syrup
- Treacle
- Jams and marmalade
- Pure oils and fats
- Vinegars
- Tomato purée
- Vanilla essence and extract
- Fresh and dried yeast

Food labels

You can tell from a food label whether or not a product is gluten-free, as allergen labelling laws mean that manufacturers have to list all the ingredients in food products. Gluten-containing cereals must be declared in the ingredients list, regardless of the amount used. Using an allergy advice box is a recommendation, but not compulsory. To check whether a food product contains gluten it is best to look at both the ingredients list and the allergy advice box on the packaging.

FOODS AND DRINKS THAT MAY INCLUDE GLUTEN WITHOUT YOU REALISING IT

- Communion wafers
- Corn tortillas may also contain regular flour
- Frozen chips may be coated with flour
- Stock cubes and powder
- Vegetable soup may contain pearl barley
- Seasoning mixes
- Mustard products
- Packet suet may have flour in it to stop it sticking together
- Commercial salad dressings and mayonnaise
- Soy sauce (gluten-free brands are available)
- Dry-roasted nuts

- Pretzels
- Bombay mix
- Scotch eggs
- Food that has been deep-fried with other gluten-containing food, e.g. battered fish and chips
- Flavoured crisps
- Some fizzy drinks (alcoholic or non-alcoholic) may contain barley flour to give a cloudy appearance
- Coffee from vending machines
- Malted milk drinks
- Barley water or flavoured barley water
- Beer, lager, stout and ale

Gluten-free alternatives

In general, it is a good idea to be wary of cereals if you are following a gluten-free diet, but there are a number of naturally gluten-free varieties that are worth knowing about. These give a similar result to cooking with regular flour and cereals and will allow you to try recipes that are otherwise out of bounds. As with all other foods, it is best to approach with a degree of caution, so check the label.

NATURALLY GLUTEN-FREE CEREALS AND GRAINS

- Arrowroot
- Buckwheat flour
- Carob flour
- Chestnut flour
- Cornflour
- Gram flour (chickpea flour)
- Linseed (flaxseed)
- Lotus root flour
- Millet flour
- Polenta (ground cornmeal)
- Potato flour
- Quinoa flour
- Rice flour
- Sago
- Sorghum
- Soya flour
- Tapioca flour (cassava flour)
- Teff

What about contamination?

Unfortunately, even the tiniest amount of gluten can cause problems for people with coeliac disease. Dry gluten-containing ingredients like flour and breadcrumbs are high-risk ingredients for contamination and cross-contamination when you are producing gluten-free meals. It is a good idea to keep gluten-free foods separate in the kitchen to make sure you avoid contamination with gluten from other foods.

STEPS TO AVOID CONTAMINATION

- Clean surfaces immediately before their use
- Use clean oil for frying chips and gluten-free foods (do not reuse oil that has been used for cooking breaded or battered products)
- Keep all pans, utensils and colanders separate during food preparation and cooking
- Use a clean grill, separate toaster or toaster bags to make gluten-free toast
- Make sure that butter, spreads, jams, pickles, chutneys and sauces are not contaminated with breadcrumbs
- Use squeezy bottles to help avoid contamination through the dipping of spoons or knives

GLUTEN-FREE BAKING – A CHEF'S PRESCRIPTION

There's no doubt that gluten-free baking is challenging, but with a little practice and the right ingredients, it can also be a lot of fun and extremely satisfying. Some people may even find it difficult to taste the difference between gluten-free recipes and their conventional counterparts!

A few years ago gluten-free ingredients and products were really few and far between and difficult to get hold of. But thanks to healthfood shops, some of the supermarkets and coeliac societies such as Coeliac UK, things are really beginning to change.

An increasing number of food companies are embracing and recognising the problems that coeliac disease poses. There have been major breakthroughs in many products such as cakes, biscuits, pasta, cookies, muffins and bread, yes, bread! On the ingredients front, gluten-free flour mixes, pancake mixes and all sorts of baking products are becoming more widely available, making home cooking easier and more accessible.

The gluten in wheat flour gives bread, cakes and pastry an appealing texture. Gluten holds the gases that are produced when cakes, and particularly breads, rise. So gluten is ordinarily a major factor in giving baked products their characteristic structure. Bread made without gluten is less chewy and lacks the characteristic springy quality, while cakes and pastry can turn out drier and more crumbly. One essential ingredient in gluten-free baking is the exotic-sounding xanthan gum. It acts as a gluten replacement and helps produce great results; turn to page 17 for more about this 'magic' ingredient!

Using a blend of gluten-free flours such as rice, potato and tapioca can replicate plain flour and ingredients such as ground almonds are often used in gluten-free baking to help to develop flavour and texture. In this book I use three different flour mixes (see page 22), two of which are great for pastries and cakes, so give a lighter finished result. The third flour mix contains soya flour, which means it has a higher protein content. The soya flour mixture can cope better with yeast and help to hold the structure of the finished product, so is ideal for bread.

I have purposely steered clear of using additives that can be bought from specialist companies in these recipes. This is because I prefer not to use them and I'm sure you probably do too; some are incredibly hard to find, while others are simply just too expensive. Also, I'm not convinced that adding too many chemicals and enhancers is a good thing for the sake of that tiny bit of extra lift or slightly lighter texture.

ESSENTIAL INGREDIENTS FOR GLUTEN-FREE BAKING

An ever-increasing variety of gluten-free baking products are available from healthfood shops and in the 'free-from' aisle of major supermarkets. Some gluten-free products are also available on prescription, and these are listed in the Coeliac UK Food and Drink Directory. Certain gluten-free products help to give great results and to replicate the quality of conventional baked items. The following are all used in this book; some will be familiar and some are more specialist, but all can really make a difference to the end results of the recipes.

Gluten-free flours

Baking with gluten-free flour, and getting successful results, can initially seem a challenge, but in fact there is a range of different flours available for the gluten-free cook. These flours can produce crumbly results but in the Basics chapter (see page 22) I give three recipes for gluten-free flour mixes that give great results. These combinations are used in many of the recipes in the book, so it's worth making a batch of each, so they're ready to use when you're in the mood for baking!

These are the flours I use in the mixes:

Brown rice flour is a creamy-coloured flour that is easy to digest. It has a slightly nutty flavour and a grainy, rather heavy texture. It is usually combined with other flours for cooking because of its texture.

Chestnut flour has a mildly nutty flavour and is very fine in texture. Chestnut flour is expensive but you can use fine polenta in Gluten-Free Flour Mix B as a cheaper alternative.

Cornflour is used widely as a thickener for sauces. Cornflour is milled from maize into a fine white powder and has a bland taste which makes it ideal for baking.

Fine polenta is an Italian staple made by grinding corn to make a rich yellow flour. It has a slightly sweet flavour and can be used to make cakes as well as a gluten-free flour mix.

Fine white rice flour is milled from polished white rice. It has a light texture and a bland flavour so is great for recipes that require a light texture.

Potato flour has a distinctive potato flavour and a heavy texture. It is great for blending with other flours and a little goes a long way. Do check the date on this flour before blending, as it does not have a very long shelf life. Potato flour should not be confused with potato starch flour, which is a different product.

Soya flour is made by grinding roasted yellow soya beans. It has a pale yellow colour, a nutty taste and a high protein content. It is best combined with other flours to form an alternative to wheat flour. It is particularly good in breads, as the protein helps to produce a good texture.

Tapioca flour is made from the root of the cassava plant, which is native to the West Indies and South America. When ground, the root forms a soft, sweet, light fine white flour, making it a good addition to any gluten-free flour mix.

Other useful ingredients

Xanthan gum is produced by fermentation and is a natural type of starch. It improves the texture and shelf life of baked products. When added to gluten-free flour mixes, it replaces the gluten 'stretch factor'. It works like gluten by binding ingredients during the baking process to give a conventional texture. It can be bought at healthfood shops and larger supermarkets, and comes in a powder form which dissolves easily in water. Xanthan gum should be combined with your gluten-free flour mix before adding any liquid.

Glycerine is fabulous for keeping moisture in sponges, biscuits and cakes. It comes in liquid form and you can buy it at the supermarket.

Baking powder (see box, page 19) helps to give a light and airy texture to baked products.

Dried yeast I always use easy-blend dried yeast, normally a 7g sachet.

Egg adds great texture and helps hold the gluten-free flour together.

Cooking margarine I've tried a variety of different types but have found that Stork margarine gives the best results.

NOTES ON THE RECIPES

Here are a few things to consider before you get baking!

Gluten-free ingredients to check before use

Several ingredients are, strictly speaking, gluten-free provided they come from a source where there is no risk of contamination. They are used in recipes in this book but please always check the label before use. You can also check the Coeliac UK Food and Drink Directory for suitable gluten-free products (see contact details on page 170).

CHECK THE COELIAC UK FOOD AND DRINK DIRECTORY FOR SUITABLE PRODUCTS OF THE FOLLOWING:

- Baking powder
- Chocolate – milk, white and dark
- Cake decorations e.g. chocolate sprinkles, edible glitter
- Oats
- Marshmallows
- Custard – ready-made and powder
- Marzipan
- Meringues
- Shortbread
- Fine polenta
- Crisp puffed rice cereal
- Soft cheese

Cooking notes

- All teaspoon and tablespoon measurements are level
- A 750W microwave was used throughout
- If you are using a fan oven, please refer to the manufacturer's handbook for the correct oven temperature conversion

How long do the products last?

Many of the cakes, biscuits and breads in the book can be frozen and each recipe has freezing instructions, along with storage instructions. An extra tip I've got to share is that warming gluten-free products, including biscuits, in a microwave for a few seconds or gently in a warm oven for a very short time makes them soft and pliable again.

And for the very best results...

Finally, after lots of testing, testing and testing again, I have found that it's critical that the recipes are adhered to exactly when measuring out all the ingredients, following the method and using the cooking instructions.

I know you will be as delighted with the results of these recipes as I have been – so now it's time to get into the kitchen, start cooking and enjoy!

BASICS

GLUTEN-FREE FLOUR MIXES

I use three Gluten-Free Flour Mixes in this book, simply because different combinations of flour work better for different recipes. Gluten-Free Flour Mixes A and B work well for biscuits and cakes, while the Gluten-Free Bread Mix contains soya flour which has a high protein content and helps most of the recipes with yeast. Make sure you check the 'best before' date of all the flours you are using, make a note of the soonest date and use the flour before then.

GLUTEN-FREE FLOUR MIX A

MAKES: 1KG
PREPARATION: 5 MINUTES

700g fine white rice flour

200g potato flour

100g tapioca flour

Mix all the flours together very thoroughly or put into a food processor and pulse until mixed. Store in an airtight container.

GLUTEN-FREE BREAD MIX

MAKES: 1.3KG
PREPARATION: 5 MINUTES

400g soya flour

200g tapioca flour

400g potato flour

300g cornflour

Mix all the flours together very thoroughly or put into a food processor and pulse until mixed. Store in an airtight container.

GLUTEN-FREE FLOUR MIX B

MAKES: 1KG
PREPARATION: 5 MINUTES

300g fine polenta (see box, page 19) or chestnut flour

500g brown rice flour

200g cornflour

Mix all the flours together very thoroughly or put into a food processor and pulse until mixed. Store in an airtight container.

SHORTBREAD PASTRY

This recipe works well as a base for a bar cake or traybake, but it can also be turned into tasty biscuits to nibble with a cup of tea.

MAKES: ONE 22CM SQUARE
SHORTBREAD BASE OR
APPROXIMATELY 12–14 BISCUITS
PREPARATION: 10 MINUTES
COOKING: 15–20 MINUTES

100g cornflour

100g rice flour

50g golden caster sugar

30g light muscovado or
soft light brown sugar

120g unsalted butter, cubed

cornflour, for dusting

demerara or caster sugar, for
sprinkling on biscuits

Preheat the oven to 190°C/gas mark 5.

Put the flours and sugars into a food processor and blend together. Add the butter and pulse until the mixture starts to clump together.

For a shortbread base: Line a 22cm square tin with baking parchment. Tip the crumb mixture into the tin and press very lightly to make an even layer. Cook the base in the oven for about 15 minutes or until pale golden brown.

For shortbread biscuits: Press the crumbs lightly into a dough and roll out thickly on a cornflour-dusted board. Press or cut into shape, transfer to a non-stick baking tray or a baking tray lined with baking parchment and bake for 12–14 minutes. Allow to cool on the tray and sprinkle with demerara or caster sugar, to serve.

☐ **TO STORE:** The base and biscuits will keep for up to 1 week in an airtight container.

✳ **TO FREEZE:** Wrap well and freeze in an airtight container. Defrost to room temperature before using.

SHORTCRUST PASTRY

In *Seriously Good! Gluten-free Cooking* I gave a recipe for pastry. Here is another version, but this time I have added a teaspoon of xanthan gum, an egg and slightly more water, which really makes a big difference to the end result. If you don't have xanthan gum you can substitute two teaspoons of psyllium husk (both are available from healthfood shops), but if using the latter you will need to add a little more water, as the absorption rate is higher.

MAKES: ONE 4CM DEEP, 24CM
ROUND TART OR FLAN CASE
PREPARATION: 10 MINUTES
COOKING: 15–20 MINUTES

225g Gluten-Free Flour Mix A
   (see page 22)

1 teaspoon xanthan gum

2 pinches of salt

110g cooking margarine

1 medium egg, beaten, at room
   temperature

Place the flour, xanthan gum and salt in a mixing bowl and mix really well. Add the margarine and rub in until you have achieved the consistency of fine breadcrumbs. I tend to take the lazy route and use a food processor. Add the egg and a little water and mix really well. Keep an eye on the texture – you may need to add a little more water so it is nice and soft; bear in mind the xanthan gum will tighten up the mixture considerably. Roll out and use as required.

To make a pastry case: Roll out the pastry, to a circle approximately 30cm in diameter, on a cornflour-dusted work surface. Transfer the pastry to a 4cm deep, 24cm round tin and line with baking parchment and baking beans.

Cook for 10 minutes at 180°C/gas mark 4, then reduce the temperature to 160°C/gas mark 3 for 10–15 minutes.

Lift out the baking parchment and beans carefully, brush thickly with beaten egg, covering any cracks, and return to the oven for 5–6 minutes to just set the egg. Brush with egg again and bake for a further 5 minutes.

☐ **TO STORE:** Wrap the dough in clingfilm and refrigerate for up to 2 days.

✳ **TO FREEZE:** Not suitable.

TUILE BISCUITS

This is the classic biscuit chefs serve with ice creams and sorbets. They are very easy to make, and look quite professional. The two-stage cooking process ensures a nice even colour to the biscuit.

These can be cooked and pressed over the bottom of an upturned tea cup or mug to make decorative cases to hold mousses, ice creams and sorbets. The uncooked mixture will keep, covered in the fridge, for a couple of weeks.

MAKES: ABOUT 12–14 BISCUITS
PREPARATION: 10 MINUTES
COOKING: 15 MINUTES

---

2 small egg whites, at room
   temperature

80g icing sugar, sieved

70g Gluten-Free Flour Mix A
   (see page 22)

70g unsalted butter, melted

Place the egg whites, icing sugar and flour into a bowl and whisk together. Add the warm melted butter and again whisk well. Chill in the fridge for at least 2 hours.

When you are ready to cook the biscuits, preheat the oven to 180°C/gas mark 4. Line a baking tray with baking parchment (you will need to cook these in batches).

Spoon out about a teaspoon-sized blob of the mixture onto the tray and spread it out as thinly as possible with a palette knife; you may only get 2–3 to a tray, as the mixture will expand. Cook until the biscuits are just set but have no colour – this is called poaching.

Remove the tray from the oven and leave the biscuits to cool for about 5 minutes. Then re-cook the biscuits for 2–3 minutes until they are a nice golden colour.

Remove the tray from the oven and using a palette knife quickly and carefully lift off the biscuits and lay them over a rolling pin, placed on a tea towel to stop it moving, to cool. You have to be quick at this point or the biscuits will set and crack very quickly. The size is up to you – I think the bigger the better!

☐ **TO STORE:** Carefully transfer the cooled biscuits to an airtight container for up to 1 week, taking care as they are quite fragile.

✱ **TO FREEZE:** Not suitable.

VANILLA CUPCAKES

Cupcakes are all the rage at the moment, and they come in many different shapes and sizes from baby cakes to giant versions that you can fill with ice cream, like I did once on *This Morning*.

The good thing, though, is that you don't need to be a baker or experienced cook to make them! This recipe has four simple steps and hey presto, they're ready to pop into the oven. So add what you like to this basic recipe, and have a bit of fun. I think this recipe is softer and tastier than a standard sponge recipe.

MAKES: 12
PREPARATION: 15 MINUTES
COOKING: 15–20 MINUTES

180g caster sugar

2 medium eggs, at room
    temperature

1 teaspoon vanilla extract

1 teaspoon glycerine

175g Gluten-Free Flour Mix A
    (see page 22)

1½ teaspoons baking powder
    (see box, page 19)

½ teaspoon xanthan gum

130ml sunflower oil

130ml whole milk

Preheat the oven to 180°C/gas mark 4. Place 12 paper muffin cases in a muffin tray.

Place the caster sugar, eggs, vanilla and glycerine into a large mixing bowl and whisk on high speed for 4 minutes.

Meanwhile, combine the flour, baking powder and xanthan gum together and mix them really well. I find it best to sieve them a couple of times, to make sure the ingredients are fully incorporated.

Next, mix the oil and milk together in a jug.

Once the egg mixture is nice and thick, add the flour mixture and liquid. Whisk well, but don't go mad.

Divide the mixture between the muffin cases. Bake for 15–20 minutes, or until well risen to the top of the paper cases. Remove the cakes, in the paper cases, from the tin and allow to cool on a wire rack.

Ice and decorate however you like.

Try a different flavour...

Add any of the following to the egg mixture with the flour: 50g dried fruit, 75g fresh berries, 50g chopped plain chocolate, 50g chopped nuts, zest of 1 lemon or 1 orange.

☐ **TO STORE:** Store in an airtight container for up to 1 week.

✳ **TO FREEZE:** Once cooled, store either in a plastic bag or an airtight container.

LIGHT SPONGE

This is a variation on a basic sponge recipe. It can be served whole, drizzled with your favourite icing, or cut into individual pieces and iced and decorated with sweets, chocolate buttons, edible glitter... the choices are endless!

Making sure the margarine and eggs are at room temperature and the milk is warmed with the glycerine will ensure the maximum lift from the sponge when cooking. The addition of glycerine helps to retain moisture in the cake's structure. I use disposable foil trays to cook this sponge, then carefully wash them and use again.

MAKES: ONE 22 X 12CM CAKE
PREPARATION: 15 MINUTES
COOKING: 20-30 MINUTES

___

vegetable oil, for oiling

175g Gluten-Free Flour Mix A
  (see page 22)

1 teaspoon bicarbonate of soda

1 teaspoon baking powder
  (see box, page 19)

85g cooking margarine

140g caster sugar

2 medium eggs, at room
  temperature

125ml semi-skimmed milk,
  warmed with 1 teaspoon
  glycerine

Preheat the oven to 160°C/gas mark 3. Lightly oil a 22 x 12cm loaf tin.

Place the flour, bicarbonate of soda and baking powder into a bowl and mix well.

Warm a large mixing bowl under hot, running water. Place the margarine and sugar in the bowl and beat until light and creamy (warming the bowl makes it easier to cream the margarine and sugar together).

Add the flour mixture to the margarine and sugar, along with the eggs, and mix well. Add the warm milk and glycerine and mix to a batter consistency, then spoon or pour into the prepared tin.

Cook for 20–25 minutes or until risen and lightly coloured. Remove and cool on a wire rack.

Ice and decorate however you like.

☐ **TO STORE:** Store in an airtight container for 2–3 days.

✱ **TO FREEZE:** Either freeze the un-iced cake whole or cut into pieces and wrap well in clingfilm.

CLASSIC PANCAKES

Everyone likes a pancake and I have had many requests for a gluten-free version. So here is a good base recipe that I first cooked on *This Morning*.

MAKES: 4–6 PANCAKES
PREPARATION: 15 MINUTES
COOKING: 6–8 MINUTES

90g brown rice flour

35g cornflour

pinch of salt

2 medium eggs, at room
  temperature

approximately 200ml
  semi-skimmed milk

3 tablespoons vegetable oil

To make the pancakes, stir the brown rice flour, cornflour and salt together in a medium mixing bowl. Add the eggs and three-quarters of the milk and whisk well until thoroughly combined. The mixture should be a similar consistency to thick double cream; add more milk if necessary.

Heat the vegetable oil in a 23cm non-stick frying pan, over a medium heat. Add 4 tablespoons of batter to the pan and swirl it around to coat the base. Cook for 30–60 seconds, then start to loosen the edges of the pancake with a palette knife. Once the pancake is set, turn it over, using the palette knife (or you can flip it in the air if you're feeling brave!) and cook the second side for 30–60 seconds or until golden brown. Repeat until all the batter is used up. Stack the pancakes on a plate as you go and cover them with foil to keep them warm.

Serve with your preferred topping (see mine below)!

RHUBARB & CUSTARD PANCAKES

approximately 225g rhubarb,
  cut into 2cm pieces

finely grated zest and juice
  of 1 large lemon

1 vanilla pod, split

4 tablespoons caster sugar,
  plus extra to taste

225g ready-made custard
  (see box, page 19)

4–6 pancakes (see above)

Place the rhubarb in a medium pan. Add the lemon zest and juice, vanilla pod and sugar and cook over a low heat for about 15 minutes, stirring occasionally; the rhubarb will break down nicely. Keep warm, but not hot.

Warm the custard, following the pack instructions. Warm the pancakes in the microwave for 10 seconds each.

To serve, lay a warm pancake on a plate, spoon in some rhubarb, fold over and spoon over a little custard. You could add a little ice cream or a blob of cream if you really wanted to push the boat out.

☐ **TO STORE:** The plain pancakes can be stacked, wrapped in clingfilm and stored in the fridge for 3–4 days.

✻ **TO FREEZE:** Not suitable.

AMERICAN-STYLE THICK PANCAKES

I really like these thick-style pancakes – they are great for breakfast or a late brunch. I find once cooked it is best to keep them warm in a clean tea towel, then reheat them before eating (10 seconds in the microwave per pancake is plenty).

MAKES: 8–10 PANCAKES
PREPARATION: 15 MINUTES
COOKING: 25 MINUTES

120g fine rice flour

½ teaspoon baking powder (see box, page 19)

pinch of salt

1 medium egg, at room temperature

1½ tablespoons sunflower oil

50g unsalted butter, melted

284ml carton buttermilk

3 tablespoons olive oil

To make the pancakes, place the rice flour, baking powder and salt in a medium mixing bowl. Place the egg, sunflower oil, melted butter and buttermilk in a jug and whisk well together. Gradually add the wet mixture to the dry ingredients, stirring well between each addition; you should end up with a loose but thickish batter.

Heat a 23cm non-stick frying pan over a medium heat and add the olive oil.

Spoon in 4 separate tablespoons of batter to make 4 small pancakes. Cook for 2–3 minutes on each side, then flip over and cook the other side until it is light brown. Repeat until all the batter is used up. Stack the pancakes on a plate as you go and cover them with foil to keep them warm.

Topping ideas
- Maple syrup and blueberries
- Golden syrup and whipped cream
- Crème fraîche and brown sugar
- Crushed bananas and peanut butter

☐ **TO STORE:** The plain pancakes can be stacked, wrapped in clingfilm and stored in the fridge for 2 days.

✳ **TO FREEZE:** Not suitable.

YORKSHIRE PUDDINGS

I often use a muffin tray to cook Yorkshire puddings because they are slightly deeper, helping to give the puddings more structure when cooked. I have also found that cooking these in a black, non-stick Yorkshire pudding tin makes them rise further than when they're cooked in a plain tin.

MAKES: 10–12
PREPARATION: 15 MINUTES
COOKING: 20–25 MINUTES

10–12 tablespoons olive oil

135g Gluten-Free Flour Mix A
  (see page 22)

140g cornflour

4 medium eggs, at room
  temperature

300ml semi-skimmed milk

salt and freshly ground
  black pepper

Preheat the oven to 220°C/gas mark 7.

Place a tablespoon of olive oil into each of 10–12 hole muffin moulds or patty tins. Place the tray on a second baking tray and pop it into the oven for 10 minutes to heat up.

Meanwhile, place the flour and cornflour in a deep mixing bowl. Add the eggs and milk and whisk until well blended. Add a little salt and pepper. Pour into the oiled moulds or tins so that they are just over half full, and return to the oven. Cook for 20–25 minutes, or until well risen and nicely browned. Serve immediately.

☐ **TO STORE:** Not suitable.

✳ **TO FREEZE:** Freeze the Yorkshire puddings once thoroughly cooled. Flash through a hot oven to crisp up.

BISCUITS

SOFT ZESTY LEMON FONDANT COOKIES

The zestiness of these cookies makes it for me, and making up the topping using fondant icing sugar with lemon juice gives the icing a really acidic kick. Fondant icing sugar is icing sugar with glucose added, so it sets at room temperature with a lovely shine, similar to the long iced buns you can buy at bakeries.

MAKES: 12 COOKIES
PREPARATION: 15 MINUTES
COOKING: 15–20 MINUTES

200g Gluten-Free Flour Mix A
(see page 22)

80g cooking margarine

¼ teaspoon baking powder
(see box, page 19)

pinch of salt

75g caster sugar

1 medium egg, at room
temperature

1 teaspoon glycerine

zest and juice of 1 large lemon

50g fondant icing sugar

extra lemon zest, to decorate

Place the flour, margarine, baking powder, salt and sugar into a food processor and blitz until you have achieved the consistency of fine breadcrumbs. Add the egg, glycerine and lemon zest and mix. Lightly bring together on a floured surface, and then form into a 15–20cm long sausage. Wrap in clingfilm and chill well.

Preheat the oven to 200°C/gas mark 6. Line two baking trays with baking parchment (you will need to cook these in batches).

When you are ready to bake the cookies, cut off 5–8mm slices of the dough and place them on the lined trays. Bake for 15–20 minutes or until cooked and lightly browned. Then transfer to a wire rack to cool.

Meanwhile, place the lemon juice in a small bowl, then add the fondant icing sugar and beat until smooth. You may need to adjust the consistency with a little water (softer) or extra fondant icing sugar (firmer). Coat the cookies thickly with the icing, decorate with lemon zest and leave to set.

☐ **TO STORE:** Store the cooled biscuits in an airtight container for up to 1 week.

✳ **TO FREEZE:** The dough and the cooked un-iced cookies freeze well.
For the dough: Wrap it in clingfilm and freeze. Defrost for 1 hour or until soft enough to cut and cook as above.
For the cookies: Wrap well and store in an airtight container. Defrost for 30 minutes, then heat through at 180°C/gas mark 4 for 2–3 minutes to soften again. Ice once cooled.

SOFT PINE NUT COOKIES

I spent a few years working in northern Italy, and every couple of weeks we would go to a pesto factory in Asti where I was helping develop recipes. We would pass a very small bakery on the way to the factory in the mornings. In the window they had many breads and cakes, but in one corner there were small meringue biscuits, which were delicious. Here is my version, light and packed full of flavour.

MAKES: ABOUT 20
PREPARATION: 15 MINUTES
COOKING: 30 MINUTES

200g flaked almonds

100g pine nuts

100g rice flour

225g caster sugar

zest of 1 lemon

2 medium egg whites,
   at room temperature

pinch of cream of tartar

½ teaspoon vanilla extract

½ teaspoon almond extract

cinnamon and sieved icing
   sugar, for dusting

Preheat the oven to 180°C/gas mark 4. Line a baking tray with baking parchment.

Place the almonds and pine nuts on the lined tray, and brown them well in the oven for 8–10 minutes; the almonds will brown slightly quicker. Once browned, remove from the oven and cool. Reduce the oven temperature to 160°C/gas mark 3.

Once cooled, place the almonds and rice flour in a food processor and blitz until you have a fine mix. Place into a medium mixing bowl, add the pine nuts, 115g of the sugar and the lemon zest, and mix well.

Whisk the egg whites with the cream of tartar until light and foamy, then add the remaining caster sugar and whisk until creamy and glossy, but do not overbeat. Mix the nut mixture into the egg whites, along with the vanilla and almond extracts.

Using two wetted teaspoons, mould the mixture into small oval mounds and place on the lined tray (you will need to cook these in batches). Pat each mound down slightly before baking. Bake for 15–20 minutes until they turn light golden, keeping an eye on them as they brown quickly. Remove and transfer to a wire rack to cool.

Sprinkle with cinnamon and icing sugar.

☐ **TO STORE:** Store the cooled biscuits in an airtight container for up to 1 week.

✱ **TO FREEZE:** Freeze the cooled cookies before dusting with the sugar and cinnamon – wrap well and store in an airtight container. Defrost for 30 minutes, then heat through at 180°C/gas mark 4 for 2–3 minutes to soften again and dust with the sugar and cinnamon.

CHOCOLATE PEANUT BUTTER & FUDGE COOKIES

This recipe is so simple it's unbelievable – just mix together well and bake! It also has the bonus of using no flour at all. If you slightly undercook the cookies you will end up with a softer, chewier texture, but if you prefer your cookies slightly crunchier, bake a little longer.

MAKES: 12–14 SOFT COOKIES
PREPARATION: 10 MINUTES
COOKING: 12–14 MINUTES

---

1 medium egg, at room temperature

80g caster sugar

125g crunchy peanut butter, at room temperature

pinch or two of chilli powder

40g hard fudge, finely chopped

40g dark chocolate (see box, page 19), finely chopped

Preheat the oven to 180°C/gas mark 4. Line two baking trays with baking parchment (you will need to cook these in batches).

Place the egg and sugar in a bowl and break up with a whisk. Add the peanut butter and chilli powder and mix well. Add the chopped fudge and chocolate and mix in.

Spoon heaped dessertspoons of the mixture onto the lined baking trays and spread out slightly, as the mixture will not spread much, then bake for 12–14 minutes.

When cooked, remove the cookies from the paper with a palette knife and cool on a wire rack.

☐ **TO STORE:** Store the cooled biscuits in an airtight container for up to 1 week.

✱ **TO FREEZE:** The cooked, cooled cookies freeze well. Wrap well and store in an airtight container. Defrost for 30 minutes, then heat through at 180°C/gas mark 4 for 2–3 minutes to soften again.

ROASTED HAZELNUT COOKIES

I love roasted hazelnuts; they make a very special cookie or shortbread and they are widely available in supermarkets. Any nut can be used instead here, but remember to roast them in the oven for an even colour rather than grilling (see method for roasting nuts in Soft Pine Nut Cookies (page 43).

MAKES: ABOUT 20
PREPARATION: 15 MINUTES
COOKING: ABOUT 10 MINUTES

115g rice flour

70g cornflour

½ teaspoon baking powder (see box, page 19)

½ teaspoon ground nutmeg

½ teaspoon mixed spice

75g stork, softened

40g caster sugar

1 tablespoon golden syrup

1 medium egg

75g roasted hazelnuts, roughly chopped

½ teaspoon xanthan gum

Preheat the oven to 180°C/gas mark 4. Line two baking trays with baking parchment (you will need to cook these in batches).

In a medium mixing bowl, combine the flours, baking powder, nutmeg and mixed spice. Mix together well. Add the stork, sugar, syrup, egg, hazelnuts and gum, and mix well.

Spoon the mixture onto the lined baking trays, using a dessertspoon to form 2–3cm rounds, spread out with a wet finger, then bake for 10 minutes or until lightly browned.

Once cooked allow the cookies to cool slightly on the trays, then transfer to a wire rack to cool completely.

☐ **TO STORE:** Store the cooled biscuits in an airtight container for up to 1 week.

✳ **TO FREEZE:** The raw dough freezes well. Wrap it in clingfilm and freeze. Defrost for 1 hour or until soft enough to cut and cook as above.

JEWELLED FLORENTINES

Delicious little treats of toasted nuts and candied fruits, caramelised into lacy biscuits and half coated in milk chocolate. Florentines make a great present at any time, or just enjoy them with a shot of espresso.

MAKES: ABOUT 12–14
PREPARATION: 20 MINUTES
COOKING: 10 MINUTES

25g unsalted butter

75g golden caster sugar

2 teaspoons clear honey

1 tablespoon rice flour

25g mixed candied peel, chopped

50g mixed glacé cherries, halved

25g dried cranberries or dried
   apricots, chopped

50g toasted flaked almonds

150g milk chocolate
   (see box, page 19)

Preheat the oven to 180°C/gas mark 4. Line two baking trays with baking parchment (you will need to cook these in batches).

Place the butter, sugar and honey in a medium non-stick pan set over a low heat. When the butter has melted, add the flour, and keep stirring for about 3 minutes, until the mixture has melted to a smooth, golden paste. Remove the pan from the heat and fold in the fruit and nuts.

Use a couple of teaspoons to shape the mixture into small heaps on the baking trays. Space out to allow for spreading and then flatten each one slightly. Bake for about 8–10 minutes, until they are a mid-golden caramel colour.

Leave the biscuits to harden and cool on the baking sheet for about 10–15 minutes, then transfer them to a wire rack.

Melt the chocolate in the microwave, or in a heatproof bowl set over a pan of just simmering water – don't let the bowl touch the water – and stir until smooth. Use a teaspoon to coat the flat side of each Florentine with warm, melted chocolate. Just before the chocolate sets, pull a fork through in a wavy line to make a pattern on the underside.

☐ **TO STORE:** Pack the cold Florentines between layers of baking parchment and pop into an airtight container for up to 1 week.

✱ **TO FREEZE:** Not suitable.

WHITE CHOC CHIP & APPLE COOKIES

This is a simple recipe and so good to eat! The white chocolate really helps to bring out the flavour of the apple and also helps with the setting of the biscuits. The grated apple needs to be squeezed out really well to get the best results. If the apple turns slightly brown don't worry, I think it adds a nice colour to the cookies.

MAKES: 12 SMALL COOKIES
PREPARATION: 15 MINUTES
COOKING: 15–20 MINUTES

100g cooking margarine

200g Gluten-Free Flour Mix A
   (see page 22)

¼ teaspoon baking powder
   (see box, page 19)

100g caster sugar

2 large pinches ground ginger

1 medium egg, at room
   temperature

1 medium Bramley apple, grated
   and thoroughly squeezed out

60g white chocolate (see box,
   page 19), finely chopped

Place the margarine, flour, baking powder, sugar and ginger into a food processor and blitz well. Add the egg and bring together, then transfer to a medium mixing bowl. Add the squeezed-out apple and chopped chocolate, and mix really well. Roll the dough into a 15–20cm long sausage shape, then wrap in clingfilm and chill for 15 minutes.

Preheat the oven to 200°C/gas mark 6. Line two baking trays with baking parchment (you will need to cook these in batches).

Scoop off 5–8mm thick sections of the chilled dough roll with a palette knife or spoon (you won't get neat slices because the dough will still be quite soft).

Place the cookies on the lined trays and bake in the oven for 15–20 minutes, or until lightly browned.

Once cooked, allow the cookies to cool slightly on the trays, then transfer to a wire rack to cool completely.

☐ **TO STORE:** Store the cooled biscuits in an airtight container for up to 1 week.

✱ **TO FREEZE:** The dough and the cooked cookies freeze well.
For the dough: Wrap it in clingfilm and freeze. Defrost for 1 hour or until soft enough to cut and cook as above.
For the cookies: Wrap well and store in an airtight container. Defrost for 30 minutes, then heat through at 180°C/gas mark 4 for 2–3 minutes to soften again.

SWEET POTATO THINS

It's not often you use sweet potato in cakes or biscuits, but the sweet flavour and texture make a great cookie and it also works well in cakes.

I add a little baking powder to lighten the texture of the biscuit, but the end result should be thin and crisp.

MAKES: 8–10
PREPARATION: 15 MINUTES
COOKING: 1 HOUR 10 MINUTES

---

1 large sweet potato, approximately 100g

150g Gluten-Free Flour Mix A (see page 22)

1 teaspoon baking powder (see box, page 19)

pinch of salt

40g caster sugar

50g cooking margarine

1 medium egg, at room temperature

sieved icing sugar and ground allspice, for dusting

Preheat the oven to 160°C/gas mark 3.

Bake the sweet potato for 50 minutes until soft. Cool slightly, then peel and mash with a fork. Set the mash aside to cool completely.

Place the flour, baking powder, salt, sugar and margarine into a medium mixing bowl and gently rub together, or place in a food processor and pulse until you have achieved the consistency of fine breadcrumbs. Add the egg and cold sweet potato and mix well. Then roll the dough into a 15–20cm long sausage and chill in the fridge for at least 1 hour.

When the dough is chilled, and you are ready to cook the biscuits, line a baking tray with baking parchment (you will need to cook these in batches).

Cut the dough into 5mm slices and place on the tray. Flatten out with your fingers until about 3mm thick, or thinner if possible. Bake for 18–20 minutes, or until lightly browned and crisp, then leave to cool on the tray or on a wire rack.

Serve dusted with icing sugar and ground allspice.

☐ **TO STORE:** Store the cooled biscuits in an airtight container for up to 1 week.

✳ **TO FREEZE:** The raw dough freezes well. Wrap it in clingfilm and freeze. Defrost for 1 hour or until soft enough to cut and cook as above.

ZESTY ORANGE & ALMOND TUILES

These nice light crispy biscuits are great to serve with ice cream and sorbets. They also look very decorative.

MAKES: ABOUT 20
PREPARATION: 10 MINUTES
COOKING: 25 MINUTES

80g icing sugar, sieved

2 medium egg whites, at room temperature

1 egg yolk, at room temperature

25g Gluten-Free Flour Mix A (see page 22)

35g chopped or flaked almonds

25g unsalted butter, melted

zest of 1 large orange

Place the sugar, egg whites, yolk, flour and almonds into a bowl and mix well. Carefully add the melted butter and orange zest and stir well. Chill in the fridge, preferably overnight, but if you cannot wait, 3 hours minimum.

Preheat the oven to 180°C/gas mark 4. Line two baking trays with baking parchment (you will need to cook these in batches).

Spoon dessertspoons of the mixture onto the baking trays, and spread out with fingers wetted in cold water. Spread as thinly as possible (do not worry about any small holes), the thinner the better. Cook in the oven until the outsides of the biscuits start to turn a pale amber colour, then remove the trays from the oven and allow the tuiles to cool. This is called poaching and ensures that the tuiles cook evenly. If you cook the tuiles for longer, the outsides will burn before the inside is cooked.

When the tuiles are completely cool, return the trays to the oven and cook for 2–3 minutes until they are a pale golden colour.

When cooked, remove from the paper with a palette knife and lay over a rolling pin to set and cool (see picture on page 26). You may find that not all of the tuiles cook at the same time, so remove the cooked tuiles one at a time, and return the trays to the oven so the others finish cooking.

☐ **TO STORE:** Carefully transfer the cooled tuiles to an airtight container (or they will go soft very quickly) for up to 1 week, taking care as they are quite fragile.

✳ **TO FREEZE:** Not suitable.

CUPCAKES & MUFFINS

HONEY MADELEINES WITH CHOCOLATE DIP

Madeleines are a traditional sweet soft French fancy. In France they use a whisked sponge method, but here I'm using a beaten method, which works extremely well. Make sure you beat the mixture until very light and creamy before adding the egg. The sponge is flavoured with a touch of honey, and the finished cakes are half dipped in chocolate and eaten warm or set – fabulous! Madeleines are perfect as an afternoon snack or you could serve them with coffee after a meal.

MAKES: 12
PREPARATION: 10 MINUTES
COOKING: 12–15 MINUTES

vegetable oil, for oiling

75g caster sugar

1 tablespoon clear honey

120g cooking margarine,
   at room temperature

1 medium egg, beaten,
   at room temperature

1 teaspoon glycerine

75g Gluten-Free Flour Mix A
   (see page 22)

½ teaspoon baking powder
   (see box, page 19)

150g dark chocolate
   (see box, page 19)

Preheat the oven to 180°C/gas mark 4. Thoroughly oil a 12-hole patty tin.

In a medium bowl, whisk the sugar, honey and margarine together really well, until very light and creamy. Gradually add the beaten egg and glycerine, stirring well after each addition. Then add the flour and baking powder and mix well.

Spoon the mixture into the prepared tins and bake for 12–15 minutes, until well risen and well browned. Remove the cakes from the tins and cool on a wire rack.

Melt the chocolate in the microwave, or in a heatproof bowl set over a pan of just simmering water – don't let the bowl touch the water – and stir until smooth.

Dip half of each sponge into the melted chocolate, then serve immediately or allow to set on clingfilm or a sheet of baking parchment.

☐ **TO STORE:** Store in an airtight container for up to 1 week.

✶ **TO FREEZE:** Once cooled and before dipping in chocolate, freeze either in a plastic bag or an airtight container. Defrost and dip in chocolate as above, before serving.

TOFFEE CHOCOLATE FUDGE BROWNIE MUFFINS

These really are wicked – gooey, sticky muffins, full of chocolate and caramel! The best thing to do is to leave them slightly undercooked, so you still have a squidgy chocolatey caramel centre. Great warm on their own, or with ice cream.

MAKES: 12
PREPARATION: 20 MINUTES
COOKING: 20 MINUTES

180g Gluten-Free Flour Mix A
 (see page 22)

50g dark muscovado sugar

50g caster sugar

20g cocoa powder

2 teaspoons baking powder
 (see box, page 19)

1 medium egg, at room
 temperature

1 teaspoon vanilla extract

400g dulce de leche, from
 a jar or tin

30g each of dark, milk and
 white chocolate (see box,
 page 19), chopped

Preheat the oven to 180°C/gas mark 4. Place 12 paper muffin cases in a muffin tray.

Place the flour, sugars, cocoa and baking powder in a bowl and mix together well. Next place the egg, vanilla extract and half the dulce de leche in a separate bowl and mix together well.

Add the egg mixture to the flour and sugar and mix well, then add the chopped chocolate and the rest of the dulce de leche and carefully 'chop' through with a spoon, leaving the mixture roughly combined. Spoon into the muffin cases and bake in the oven for 18–20 minutes.

Remove when well risen and still slightly undercooked. Cool slightly on a wire rack and eat warm or cold.

☐ **TO STORE:** Store in an airtight container for up to 1 week.

✳ **TO FREEZE:** Once cooled, freeze either in a plastic bag or an airtight container. Defrost for 1 hour, then warm each muffin through for 10 seconds in the microwave on full power.

BUTTERMILK BREAKFAST MUFFINS

A tasty twist on a much used format, here the frozen blueberries defrost perfectly when cooking, leaving little pockets of brilliantly purple juice. Don't restrict yourself to blueberries though – any frozen berries will work.

Soaking the oats in buttermilk first really helps to keep the muffins moist. Buttermilk is the by-product when butter is produced; it has a slight acidic edge to it and this, coupled with the bicarbonate of soda and baking powder, causes a slight chemical reaction, producing bubbles of air to increase the lift in the end result – all clever stuff! Most supermarkets sell buttermilk now.

MAKES: 12 MUFFINS
PREPARATION: 15 MINUTES
COOKING: 15–20 MINUTES

200g porridge oats
   (see box, page 19)

284ml carton buttermilk

125g caster sugar

150ml vegetable oil

1 medium egg, at room
   temperature

1 tablespoon glycerine

200g Gluten-Free Flour Mix A
   (see page 22)

1½ teaspoon baking powder
   (see box, page 19)

½ teaspoon xanthan gum

½ teaspoon bicarbonate of soda

75g frozen blueberries

Preheat the oven to 200°C/gas mark 6. Place 12 paper muffin cases in a muffin tray.

Place the oats, buttermilk and sugar in a medium mixing bowl and set aside for 20 minutes.

Whisk the oil, egg and glycerine together in a jug and add to the oat mixture. Then stir in the flour, baking powder, xanthan gum and bicarbonate of soda. Finally add the blueberries and mix well.

Spoon into the muffin cases and cook for 15 minutes or until well browned and risen.

Cool on a wire rack and serve.

☐ **TO STORE:** Store in an airtight container for up to 1 week.

✳ **TO FREEZE:** Once cooled, freeze either in a plastic bag or an airtight container.

EASY APRICOT & BRANDY PAN MUFFIN

Muffins are generally made in small cases and baked individually. But this is a fruity muffin recipe with a difference – all you need is an ovenproof non-stick frying pan to cook it in!

A couple of good tips here: make sure the margarine and eggs are at room temperature (warming the mixing bowl makes it easier to cream them together too). And warm the milk with the glycerine. This will ensure the mixture won't curdle or split, making a lighter, more even-textured sponge. It will also ensure the maximum lift from the sponge when cooking. Glycerine helps to retain moisture in the cake's structure; something that's essential when cooking without gluten.

MAKES: ONE 25CM ROUND, 5CM DEEP MUFFIN
PREPARATION: 15 MINUTES
COOKING: 20–30 MINUTES

175g Gluten-Free Flour Mix A (see page 22)

1 teaspoon bicarbonate of soda

1 teaspoon baking powder (see box, page 19)

85g cooking margarine, at room temperature

140g caster sugar

2 medium eggs, at room temperature

125ml semi-skimmed milk, warmed with 1 teaspoon glycerine

2–3 tablespoons brandy

2 tablespoons vegetable oil

2 x 420g cans apricots in syrup, drained (approximately 280g of fruit)

Preheat the oven to 180°C/gas mark 4.

Place the flour, bicarbonate of soda and baking powder in a medium bowl and mix well.

Warm a large mixing bowl under hot running water. Place the margarine and sugar in the bowl and beat them together until light and creamy.

Add the flour mixture and eggs to the creamed mixture and stir well. Then add the warm milk, glycerine and brandy, and mix to a batter consistency.

Heat a 25 × 5cm deep non-stick ovenproof frying pan over a medium heat, and add the oil. Arrange the apricots evenly in the pan, round side down, cut side up. Spoon the mixture over the fruit evenly, then with a palette knife or the back of a tablespoon, spread it over the fruit to even it out.

Bake in the oven for 20–25 minutes or until risen and lightly coloured.

Remove and cool in the pan for 5 minutes, then invert the muffin onto a wire rack to cool completely. To serve, transfer it to a plate and cut it into wedges.

☐ **TO STORE:** Store, whole or cut into wedges, in an airtight container for up to 1 week.

✳ **TO FREEZE:** Freeze on the serving plate, wrapped in foil.

SWEET COURGETTE & SAFFRON BUTTERFLY CAKES

When I was a child my mum would make butterfly cakes, and I still love them! The addition of grated courgettes and saffron gives a lovely soft edge to these buns. Good old-fashioned buttercream (now more commonly known as frosting) is a lovely way to finish them.

MAKES: 12
PREPARATION: 20 MINUTES
COOKING: 15–20 MINUTES

---

1 good pinch saffron threads or powder

2 tablespoons boiling water

2 medium eggs, at room temperature

180g caster sugar

200g Gluten-Free Flour Mix A (see page 22)

2 teaspoons baking powder (see box, page 19)

½ teaspoon xanthan gum

1 teaspoon glycerine

2 medium courgettes, grated and thoroughly squeezed out (approximately 240g)

225g unsalted butter, softened

70g icing sugar, sieved

sieved icing sugar, to dust

Preheat the oven to 180°C/gas mark 4. Place 12 paper muffin cases in a muffin tray.

Place the saffron stems or powder in a mug, add the boiling water and leave to infuse and cool.

Next, place the eggs and sugar into a food mixer and whisk over a high speed for 5 minutes, or until thick and creamy.

Place the flour, baking powder and xanthan gum together in another bowl and mix well.

Once the egg and sugar are very thick, add the saffron water, the glycerine, the flour mix and the courgettes. Fold together well, then spoon into the muffin cases.

Bake for 15–20 minutes until slightly brown and well risen. Remove and allow to cool completely on a wire rack.

To make the buttercream, beat the butter and icing sugar together in a medium bowl.

Once the cakes are cold, cut out a small fairly deep circle of sponge from the top of each cake with a sharp knife, then cut each circle in half. Spoon a little frosting into the hole in the sponge, then invert the two half circles of sponge and stick onto the frosting to look like butterfly wings.

Dust with icing sugar and serve.

For a splash more colour

Try adding a little infused saffron (1 small pinch of saffron threads or powder infused in 2 teaspoons boiling water) to the buttercream for extra colour.

☐ **TO STORE:** Store, un-iced, in an airtight container for up to 1 week.

✱ **TO FREEZE:** Once cooled, freeze the un-iced cakes in a plastic bag or airtight container.

COFFEE CUPCAKES WITH MOCHA FONDANT ICING

The icing here is delicious, and makes these really special. I use fondant icing sugar, which is available from supermarkets and is great because it doesn't need to be sieved.

MAKES: 12 CAKES
PREPARATION: 10 MINUTES
COOKING: 20 MINUTES

For the cakes

175g Gluten-Free Flour Mix A or B (see page 22)

1½ teaspoons baking powder (see box, page 19)

½ teaspoon xanthan gum

175g caster sugar

2 medium eggs, at room temperature

1 teaspoon vanilla extract

1 teaspoon glycerine

125ml semi-skimmed milk

125ml sunflower oil

2 tablespoons instant coffee dissolved in 1 tablespoon boiling water

For the mocha fondant icing

1 tablespoon instant coffee and 2 teaspoons cocoa powder dissolved in 2 tablespoons boiling water

150g fondant icing sugar

Preheat the oven to 180°C/gas mark 4. Place 12 paper muffin cases in a muffin tray.

Mix the flour, baking powder and xanthan gum together.

Place the caster sugar, eggs, vanilla and glycerine in another mixing bowl and, using a hand-held electric mixer, whisk on high speed for a couple of minutes until thick and double in volume. When the eggs are nice and thick, fold in the flour mix.

Next mix the milk and the oil with the coffee liquid in a jug. Start whisking on low speed and slowly pour the liquid into the cake batter; whisk well but don't go mad. It will still seem quite wet. Divide the batter between the 12 cases, filling them about halfway.

Bake for about 20 minutes, or until well risen and a skewer inserted into the centre comes out clean. Remove and allow to cool completely on a wire rack.

To make the icing, mix the mocha liquid gradually into the fondant icing sugar; add more or less liquid to form a thick paste. Spread the icing onto the centre of each cold cake and coax it to the sides. The fondant icing gives a brilliant shine to the topping for the cupcakes.

Topping variation
You could skip the cocoa in the icing, top with a glistening coffee glaze and sprinkle with some crushed walnuts for a retro coffee and walnut taste.

☐ **TO STORE:** Store, un-iced, in an airtight container for up to 1 week.

✳ **TO FREEZE:** Once cooled, freeze the un-iced cakes in a plastic bag or airtight container.

TANGY BEETROOT & BLACKCURRANT MUFFINS

The use of sweet pickled beetroot, along with the blackcurrants, makes a nice difference, giving an almost sweet and sour edge to these muffins. They are delicious served warm with a scoop of vanilla ice cream, and I have also been known to eat them warm with a slice of Gorgonzola cheese or a sliver of mature Cheddar cheese!

MAKES: 12
PREPARATION: 15 MINUTES
COOKING: 15–18 MINUTES

---

2 medium eggs, at room
  temperature

225g caster sugar

175g Gluten-Free Flour Mix A
  (see page 22)

pinch of salt

1½ teaspoons baking powder
  (see box, page 19)

130ml vegetable oil

130ml semi-skimmed milk

1 teaspoon glycerine

100g sweet pickled beetroot,
  drained and finely diced

100g frozen blackcurrants

Preheat the oven to 180°C/gas mark 4. Place 12 paper muffin cases in a muffin tray.

Whisk the eggs and sugar in a medium bowl for about 2 minutes by hand.

Mix all the dry ingredients really well together. Combine the oil, milk and glycerine in a jug. Add the dry ingredients to the beaten eggs and sugar, followed by the oil mixture, then mix well. Next stir in the beetroot and blackcurrants.

Scoop the mixture into the muffin cases, and bake for 15–18 minutes, or until well risen and cooked through. Remove and allow to cool on a wire rack.

☐ **TO STORE:** Store in an airtight container for up to 1 week.

✳ **TO FREEZE:** Once cooled, freeze in a plastic bag or airtight container.

BLUE CHEESE BUTTERMILK MUFFINS

A savoury version of the ever-popular muffin that is light, tasty and really easy to make, and they also freeze really well. You can use any blue cheese for this recipe, such as Stilton, or you could try dolcelatte for a lighter texture. You can get buttermilk from most supermarkets now.

MAKES: 10 MUFFINS
PREPARATION: 15 MINUTES
COOKING: 20–25 MINUTES

225g Gluten-Free Flour Mix B
    (see page 22)

2 teaspoons baking powder
    (see box, page 19)

pinch of celery salt

50g blue cheese, crumbled or
    finely chopped

small handful of fresh basil
    leaves, snipped

175ml semi-skimmed milk

100ml buttermilk

50g unsalted butter, melted

1 large egg, at room
    temperature

Preheat the oven to 200°C/gas mark 6. Prepare a muffin tray: cut 10 squares of greaseproof paper to fit each hole, with the edges overlapping or line with 10 paper muffin cases.

Sieve the flour into a large bowl with the baking powder and celery salt. Stir in the cheese and the basil.

In a large jug, beat the milks, melted butter and egg together with a hand-held electric whisk.

Make a well in the centre of the dry ingredients and gradually add the liquid ingredients. The mixture should be soft, but not too thick. Immediately spoon the mixture into the muffin papers, filling them about halfway.

Bake for 20–25 minutes, or until well risen and golden. Remove and eat when just cooled from the oven or allow to cool on a wire rack.

Variation
For an extra burst of flavour add 5–6 sun-dried tomatoes from a jar of oil. Drain well, finely chop and add to the mixture at the same time as the cheese.

☐ **TO STORE:** Store in an airtight container for up to 1 week. Warm the cold muffins for a few seconds in a microwave before serving.

✱ **TO FREEZE:** Once cooled, double wrap in clingfilm and freeze in an airtight container. Defrost for 1 hour and then warm each muffin through for 10 seconds in the microwave on full power.

LARGE CAKES

POLENTA CAKE WITH RASPBERRY DRIZZLE FROSTING

Polenta cakes are very trendy at the moment – there's hardly a week goes by when you don't see a recipe in the weekend newspapers. Here is a light-textured version – bear in mind the finer the polenta the smoother the texture of the cake. I quite like a grittier texture.

MAKES: ONE 20CM SQUARE CAKE
PREPARATION: 10 MINUTES
COOKING: 45–50 MINUTES

For the sponge

vegetable oil, for oiling

175g soft unsalted butter

225g caster sugar

3 medium eggs, at room temperature

150g fine polenta (see box, page 19)

100g Gluten-Free Flour Mix A (see page 22)

2 teaspoons xanthan gum

1 tablespoon glycerine

½ teaspoon baking powder (see box, page 19)

For the raspberry drizzle frosting

finely grated zest and juice of 2 large limes

250g fondant icing sugar

250g fresh or frozen raspberries

Preheat the oven to 180°C/gas mark 4. Lightly oil a 6.5cm deep, 20cm square, loose-based cake tin.

Lightly cream the butter and sugar together in a large mixing bowl. Beat in the eggs, polenta, flour, xanthan gum, glycerine and baking powder. Stir well and pour into the prepared cake tin.

Place the tin on a baking tray and cook for 40–45 minutes or until well risen and lightly browned.

Remove from the oven and allow to cool in the tin. Then remove from the tin and place on a serving plate.

For the frosting, mix the lime juice, zest and fondant icing sugar together until you have the consistency of very thick cream.

If using fresh raspberries, spoon the icing over the sponge, then place the raspberries on top. Leave the cake to set at room temperature.

If using frozen raspberries, coat the cake well in the icing, place the frozen raspberries on top and leave for 40 minutes to defrost. The juice will run into the icing and look wonderful.

☐ **TO STORE:** The un-iced cake will keep for 1 week, stored in an airtight container.

✱ **TO FREEZE:** Freeze the cake before frosting it. Wrap it well and place in an airtight container. Top with the frosting and raspberries once thawed.

FROSTED CARROT CAKE

A twist on an old favourite here; it has a really nice texture which I reckon is better than when made with ordinary flour.

MAKES: ONE 23 x 13 x 7CM LOAF
PREPARATION: 15 MINUTES
COOKING: 40–45 MINUTES

For the carrot cake

vegetable oil, for oiling

150g light muscovado sugar

125ml sunflower oil

3 medium eggs, at room temperature

225g Gluten-Free Flour Mix B (see page 22)

1 teaspoon xanthan gum

½ teaspoon bicarbonate of soda

½ teaspoon baking powder (see box, page 19)

½ teaspoon mixed spice

2 tablespoons semi-skimmed milk

250g carrots, grated

For the cinnamon frosting

200g half-fat cream cheese, at room temperature

75g icing sugar, sieved

½ teaspoon ground cinnamon

grated zest of 1 small lime or 1 small orange, plus extra to decorate

Preheat the oven to 180°C/gas mark 4. Oil a 23 × 13 × 7cm loaf tin and base-line with baking parchment.

Tip the sugar into a large mixing bowl. Using a hand-held electric mixer, whisk in the oil and the eggs, one at a time.

Sift together the flour, xanthan gum, bicarbonate of soda, baking powder and mixed spice and add this to the bowl, stirring well. Add the milk and stir well to loosen the mixture. Stir in the grated carrots and mix all the ingredients evenly.

Spoon the mixture into the prepared tin and bake for 40–45 minutes, until firm and springy in the centre and a skewer inserted into the centre comes out clean. Cool in the tin for 10 minutes. Turn the cake out of the tin, peel off the paper and allow to cool completely on a wire rack.

To make the frosting, beat all the ingredients together in a small bowl until smooth. Set the cake on a serving plate, spread the frosting over, sprinkle with the extra lime or orange zest and cut into slices to serve.

Variation: carrot cupcakes

Divide the mixture between 10–12 muffin cases, then bake for 20–25 minutes or until risen, golden and a skewer comes out clean when inserted into the centre. Allow to cool completely on a wire rack. When cool, pipe the tops with the cinnamon frosting and decorate with lime or orange zest.

☐ **TO STORE:** The iced cake keeps well for 2–3 days in an airtight container in the fridge.

✳ **TO FREEZE:** The un-iced cake freezes well. Wrap the cake in baking parchment and place it in an airtight container. Store for up to 3 months and ice the cake after defrosting.

PEAR, BLUEBERRY & POLENTA CAKE

The fruit flavours work really well in this sponge, which has an indulgent cream cheese frosting. You can use this as a basic recipe and change the fruit depending on what's in season. I've also given an alternative fondant icing topping below.

MAKES: 12 SQUARES
PREPARATION: 25 MINUTES
COOKING: 30 MINUTES

For the sponge

vegetable oil, for oiling

3 pears

finely grated zest of 1 large lemon plus 1 tablespoon lemon juice

175g unsalted butter

225g golden caster sugar

3 medium eggs, beaten, at room temperature

1 teaspoon vanilla extract

3 teaspoons baking powder (see box, page 19)

250g fine polenta (see box, page 19)

100g blueberries

For the frosting

25g butter, softened

300g half-fat cream cheese

50g icing sugar, sieved

Preheat the oven to 180°C/gas mark 4. Oil a 22cm square baking tin.

Peel and slice the pears, cut into rough chunks and coat in the lemon juice to prevent them from browning.

Place the unsalted butter and golden caster sugar in a mixing bowl and cream them together, using a hand-held electric whisk. Add the eggs, half the lemon zest, the vanilla extract, baking powder and polenta and mix well. Carefully fold in the pears. Spoon the mixture into the prepared tin and press a layer of blueberries on the top.

Bake for about 30 minutes, until well risen and golden. Test with a skewer, which should emerge clean when inserted into the centre. Remove from the oven and leave to cool in the tin.

For the frosting, put the butter and cream cheese into a medium bowl, mix until soft and smooth and then beat in the icing sugar. Remove the cake from the tin. Spread the frosting evenly over the cake and sprinkle with the reserved lemon zest. Cut into squares to serve. The cake is best eaten on the same day that you ice and decorate it.

Alternative fondant topping

Prepare the sponge as above, transfer it to the oiled tin and cook it without the blueberries. Leave to cool in the tin.

In a medium bowl, mix 4 tablespoons of lemon juice with 250g fondant icing sugar until it is the consistency of very thick cream. Remove the sponge from the tin and spoon half the icing over the cooled sponge. Top with 100g blueberries or seasonal soft fruit of your choice. Drizzle over the rest of the icing and leave to set.

☐ **TO STORE:** The un-iced cake will keep for 2 days in an airtight container.

✳ **TO FREEZE:** Not suitable.

FROSTED LEMON & LIME DRIZZLE CAKE

A great tea-time favourite! I use a lemon and lime syrup to moisten the sponge and a thin lime fondant glaze to finish the cake off, which gives a really zingy flavour.

MAKES: ONE 20CM ROUND CAKE
PREPARATION: 20 MINUTES, PLUS COOLING
COOKING: 30 MINUTES

For the cake

vegetable oil, for oiling

225g caster sugar

4 medium eggs, at room temperature

350g Gluten-Free Flour Mix B (see page 22)

1½ teaspoons xanthan gum

2 teaspoons baking powder (see box, page 19)

400ml semi-skimmed milk

200ml sunflower oil

zest and juice of 2 large lemons

For the syrup

2 large limes

75g granulated sugar

For the crunchy icing

juice of 1 large lime

100g fondant icing sugar

granulated sugar, for sprinkling

lemon and lime zest, to decorate

Preheat the oven to 180°C/gas mark 4. Oil a 20cm round, loose-based cake tin and base-line with baking parchment.

Whisk the sugar and the eggs together in a food processor until thick and creamy. Sift together the flour, xanthan gum and baking powder to combine evenly and add this to the sugar and eggs. Whisk in the milk, oil, and lemon zest (reserve the juice for the syrup).

Spoon the mixture into the prepared tin and bake for about 30 minutes, until firm and springy in the centre. Test with a skewer; if it comes out clean, it's done. The cake will be nicely browned and domed. Once cooked, remove from the oven and allow it to cool slightly in the tin.

To make the syrup, squeeze the limes and pour the juice into a measuring jug with the reserved lemon juice – you'll need approximately 120ml in total. Next, place the measured lemon and lime juice into a small pan with the granulated sugar and boil them together for 1 minute.

Prick the warm cake all over with a skewer, while it is still in the tin, then pour over the hot syrup. Once the cake is cool, carefully remove it from the tin and place it on a wire rack to cool completely.

To make the icing, place the lime juice in a small bowl and add the fondant icing sugar to form a runny icing. Sprinkle the top of the cake with a little granulated sugar. Pour the icing all over the cake and leave to run over the edge. Decorate with lemon and lime zest.

☐ **TO STORE:** The iced cake keeps well for 2 days in an airtight container in the fridge.

✳ **TO FREEZE:** The un-iced cake freezes well. Wrap the cake in baking parchment and place in an airtight container. Store for up to 3 months and finish with icing after defrosting.

APPLE PUDDING CAKE WITH CIDER CRUNCH TOPPING

This is a cross between a cake and a bread – very moist and absolutely delicious! The fruit gives it a close texture, a bit like old-fashioned bread pudding, only golden in colour.

This is a bit of a West Country treat, with the cider topping, especially if you serve it with generous dollops of clotted cream!

MAKES: ONE 20CM ROUND CAKE
PREPARATION: 20 MINUTES,
PLUS 2 HOURS SOAKING TIME
COOKING: 1 HOUR

For the cake

175g mixed dried fruit

75g sultanas

100ml dry cider

vegetable oil, for oiling

225g Gluten-Free Flour Mix A
(see page 22)

1 teaspoon xanthan gum

1 tablespoon baking powder
(see box, page 19)

2 teaspoons mixed spice

175g cooking margarine

175g soft light brown sugar

3 medium eggs, beaten, at room
temperature

3 crisp eating apples (e.g. English
Cox's or Braeburn)

For the cider crunch topping

25g demerara sugar

2 teaspoons dry cider

Place the dried fruit in a bowl and pour the cider over. Set aside for a couple of hours to macerate.

Preheat the oven to 180°C/gas mark 4. Oil a 20cm round loose-based cake tin and base-line with baking parchment.

Sift the flour with the xanthan gum, baking powder and spice. Using a hand-held electric mixer, cream the margarine and sugar together until fluffy and light. Gradually beat in the eggs along with 2 tablespoons of the flour mixture.

Next, grate one of the apples, including the skin, into the mixture, then chop a second apple into small chunks and fold them into the cake batter along with the rest of the flour mixture. Now add the soaked dried fruit and its liquid and combine the mixture evenly. Slice the remaining apple and reserve the slices to put on top.

Spoon the cake mixture into the prepared tin. Press the reserved slices of apple into the top of the cake, sprinkle with 2 teaspoons of the demerara sugar and bake for about one hour, or until well risen and a skewer inserted into the centre comes out clean. Cool in the tin for 30 minutes and turn out onto a wire rack to cool completely.

Make the cider crunch topping just before serving: mix the cider with the remaining demerara sugar to make a wet paste. Dot the crunchy paste over the cake.

☐ **TO STORE:** The cake will keep for 1 week, without the topping, in an airtight container.

✱ **TO FREEZE:** Wrap the cake, without the topping, in baking parchment and foil and freeze in an airtight container. Defrost for 1–2 hours and top with the crunchy cider topping after defrosting.

CHOCOLATE BROWNIE TORTE

Everybody likes chocolate brownies! This recipe is a variation and makes a really squidgy and rich torte.

MAKES: ONE 20CM ROUND CAKE
PREPARATION: 20 MINUTES
COOKING: 30 MINUTES, PLUS 15 MINUTES COOLING

---

vegetable oil, for oiling

275g dark chocolate (see box, page 19)

5 medium eggs, separated, at room temperature

175g golden caster sugar

140g ground almonds

sieved icing sugar, for dusting

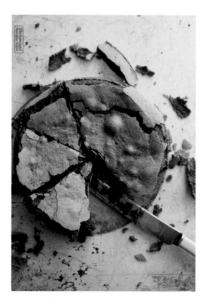

Preheat the oven to 170°C/gas mark 3. Oil a 20cm round loose-based cake tin and base-line with baking parchment.

Roughly chop 50g of the chocolate, and set aside. Melt the remaining chocolate, either in the microwave or in a heatproof bowl set over a pan of simmering water, and cool slightly.

Whisk the egg whites in a very clean bowl until they form soft peaks. Gradually whisk in half the sugar, a tablespoon at time, until incorporated and you have a soft meringue.

Using a hand-held electric whisk, beat the egg yolks together with the remaining sugar in a large mixing bowl, until pale and doubled in volume. Carefully fold half the meringue mixture into the egg yolk mixture, so you keep all the air in. Gently fold in the melted chocolate and then carefully fold in the rest of the meringue mixture. Finally fold in the ground almonds and the chopped chocolate.

Spoon the mixture into the tin, level it and bake in the centre of the oven for 30 minutes. Turn the oven off and leave the cake in there for 15 minutes – it will continue cooking as it cools. Remove the cake from the oven and leave to cool in the tin, on a wire rack.

The surface of the torte will be cracked (the cracks are part of its charm) and crusted and underneath it will be soft and moist. Dust the top with icing sugar to serve.

Variation
If you like you could add 2–3 tablespoons of orange liqueur when you add the melted chocolate to the mixture.

☐ **TO STORE:** The cake will keep for 3–4 days, in an airtight container, in the fridge.

✻ **TO FREEZE:** Wrap the un-dusted cake in baking parchment and place it in an airtight container. Defrost for 1–2 hours and then dust with icing sugar.

ROASTED BANANA WALNUT CAKE WITH MAPLE ICING

This combines some of my favourite flavours in one moist sponge cake. Made with roasted bananas for a great texture, and drizzled with a deliciously sticky maple icing – fantastic!

MAKES: ONE 23 x 13 x 7CM LOAF
PREPARATION: 15 MINUTES
COOKING: 40–50 MINUTES

For the cake

450g bananas with skin on (about 250g after roasting)

150g light muscovado sugar

125ml sunflower oil

1 teaspoon glycerine

3 medium eggs, at room temperature

225g Gluten-Free Flour Mix B (see page 22)

½ teaspoon xanthan gum

½ teaspoon bicarbonate of soda

½ teaspoon baking powder (see box, page 19)

2 tablespoons crème fraîche or cream cheese

50g walnut pieces

For the maple icing

3 tablespoons maple syrup

75g fondant icing sugar

crushed walnuts, to decorate

Preheat the oven to 200°C/gas mark 6.

Make a slit in each banana and place on a baking tray. Roast the bananas in their skins for about 10 minutes until soft. Cool, mash roughly, and set aside.

Reduce the oven temperature to 180°C/gas mark 4. Oil a 23 × 13 × 7cm loaf tin and base-line with baking parchment.

Tip the sugar into a large mixing bowl and, using a hand-held electric mixer, whisk in the oil, glycerine and eggs, one at a time.

Sift together the flour, xanthan gum, bicarbonate of soda and baking powder and mix this into the bowl, with the crème fraîche or cream cheese. Stir in 250g mashed banana and the walnuts and mix all the ingredients thoroughly.

Smooth the mixture into the prepared tin and bake for about 45 minutes until firm and springy when touched. Test with a skewer, which should come out clean when inserted into the centre. Cool in the tin for 10 minutes. Turn the cake out of the tin, peel off the paper and cool on a wire rack.

For the icing, mix the maple syrup into the fondant icing, with just enough drops of water to make a runny icing. Set the cake on a serving plate, drizzle the maple glaze over and scatter some crushed walnuts on the top. Cut into slices to serve.

☐ **TO STORE:** The un-iced cake will keep for 1 week in an airtight container.

✱ **TO FREEZE:** Wrap the un-iced cake in baking parchment and foil and freeze in an airtight container. Defrost for 1–2 hours and ice after defrosting.

PLUM & ALMOND BUTTER CAKE

This is a buttery sponge cake with moist, sweet fruit, to cut into wedges. Try it in autumn when plums are in season. Or alternatively choose cherries, peaches, nectarines or apricots in the summer months.

This cake can be warmed before serving and enjoyed as a dessert with ice cream or served cold – and it's great for picnics.

MAKES: ONE 20CM ROUND CAKE
PREPARATION: 20 MINUTES
COOKING: 40–45 MINUTES

---

vegetable oil, for oiling

3 medium eggs, at room temperature

2 teaspoons vanilla extract

125g caster sugar

200g Gluten-Free Flour Mix B (see page 22)

1 tablespoon baking powder (see box, page 19)

1 teaspoon xanthan gum

125g unsalted butter, melted

1 teaspoon glycerine

3 tablespoons semi-skimmed milk

350–400g red plums, quartered and stoned

2 tablespoons demerara sugar

125g flaked almonds

Preheat the oven to 180°C/gas mark 4. Oil a 20cm round loose-based cake tin and base-line with baking parchment.

Put the eggs into a bowl with the vanilla extract and caster sugar. Using a hand-held electric mixer, whisk until light and the mixture forms a trail. Sieve the flour with the baking powder and the xanthan gum, mix thoroughly and fold into the mixture, stirring lightly, so you don't lose all the air in the batter. Stir in the melted butter, glycerine and milk. Do not overbeat.

Put a layer of cake mixture in the base of the tin. Scatter some of the plums over, then spoon in the rest of the cake batter. Tip the remaining plums on top. Sprinkle the demerara sugar and the almonds over the fruit.

Place the cake on a baking tray and bake for about 45 minutes, until the plums have begun to caramelise and a skewer inserted into the cake comes out clean. Remove the cake from the oven, leave to cool slightly and then gently loosen the sides. Transfer to a wire rack to cool completely.

☐ **TO STORE:** The cake will keep for 1 week in an airtight container.

✳ **TO FREEZE:** Wrap the cake in baking parchment and foil, and freeze in an airtight container.

QUICK EXTRA MOIST FRUIT CAKE

One of the best pieces of advice I was ever given was to soak the fruit before making any fruit cake and then taste the difference. It makes perfect sense if you think about it – dried fruit will reconstitute during cooking, drawing moisture from the cooked sponge and making the cake dry. Soaking the fruit simply ensures you have a deliciously moist cake.

MAKES: ONE 23 x 13 x 7CM LOAF
PREPARATION: 15 MINUTES,
PLUS 2 HOURS SOAKING TIME
COOKING: 50–60 MINUTES

100g raisins

100g sultanas

75g semi-dried cranberries

125ml semi-skimmed milk,
    warmed

vegetable oil, for greasing

90g cooking margarine

125g caster sugar

180g Gluten-Free Flour Mix A
    (see page 22)

1 teaspoon bicarbonate
    of soda

1½ teaspoons baking powder
    (see box, page 19)

1 teaspoon xanthan gum

125ml semi-skimmed milk,
    warmed with 2 teaspoons
    glycerine

2 medium eggs, beaten,
    at room temperature

Place the fruit in a bowl, add the warmed milk and stir well. Leave for at least 2 hours or until the milk has been absorbed.

Preheat the oven to 160°C/gas mark 3. Oil a 23 × 13 × 7cm loaf tin and base-line with baking parchment.

Place the margarine and sugar in a mixing bowl and beat until nice and creamy. In a separate bowl, mix the flour, bicarbonate of soda, baking powder and xanthan gum really well. Add the flour mix to the margarine and sugar, then add the warm milk and glycerine and mix well. Stir in the beaten eggs. Finally add the soaked fruit and liquid and spoon into the prepared tin.

Cook in the oven for 50–60 minutes. The cake is ready when a skewer inserted into the sponge comes out clean.

Once cooked, remove from the oven and cool for 5 minutes in the tin, then transfer to a wire rack to cool completely.

☐ **TO STORE:** The cake will keep for 1 week in an airtight container.

✳ **TO FREEZE:** Wrap well in clingfilm and freeze.

CELEBRATION CAKES

VANILLA & RASPBERRY CAKE

In my book *Seriously Good! Gluten Free Cooking* there is a lovely birthday cake recipe. Since the publication of that book I have had many enquiries about children's cakes, so here is another version by special request.

MAKES: ONE 20CM ROUND
SPONGE CAKE
PREPARATION: 15 MINUTES,
PLUS COOLING AND DECORATING
COOKING: 30 MINUTES

For the sponge

vegetable oil, for greasing

350g golden caster sugar

4 medium eggs, at room
  temperature

2 teaspoons vanilla extract

2 teaspoons glycerine

350g Gluten-Free Flour Mix B
  (see page 22)

1 teaspoon xanthan gum

3 teaspoons baking powder
  (see box, page 19)

250ml semi-skimmed milk

250ml sunflower oil

For the buttercream
and decoration

225g unsalted butter,
  softened

225g icing sugar, sieved

1 teaspoon vanilla extract

fresh raspberries

4 tablespoons raspberry jam

edible glitter (see box, page 19)
  – try www.squires-shop.com

Preheat the oven to 180°C/gas mark 4. Oil two 20cm Victoria sandwich tins and base-line with baking parchment.

Place the caster sugar, eggs, vanilla and glycerine into a food mixer and whisk on high speed for 3 minutes. Sift together the flour, xanthan gum and baking powder to combine evenly. In a jug, mix the milk with the oil.

When the eggs are nice and thick, add the flour mix. Return the bowl to the mixer and slowly add the milk and the oil. Whisk thoroughly, but don't go mad.

Divide the mixture evenly between the tins and level the surface. Bake on the same shelf in the centre of the oven for 30–35 minutes until golden and firm. The cakes are ready when a skewer inserted into the sponge comes out clean.

Leave the cakes to cool in the tins for 15 minutes and then turn out onto a wire rack to cool completely.

Peel off the lining paper and decorate the cakes or freeze them (see below) until you are ready to use them.

To make the buttercream, beat the butter with the icing sugar and vanilla extract until light and fluffy.

Select the cake with the best top and set it aside. Turn the other cake over (trim the base to make it sit flat if necessary) and place it on a serving plate or cake board. Spread a layer of buttercream over the base sponge, saving a generous amount for the top. Spread the same sponge with raspberry jam and sandwich the two cakes together.

Spread the rest of the buttercream over the top of the cake. Top with fresh raspberries and sprinkle with some edible glitter. The cake is best eaten on the same day that you ice and decorate it.

Filling variations

Buttercream and jam are a classic combination for filling a sponge cake but you could also use lightly whipped cream with crushed fresh berries, or if the mood takes you, try lemon curd or marmalade and liqueur instead.

☐ **TO STORE:** The un-iced cakes will keep for 2 days in an airtight container.

✱ **TO FREEZE:** Wrap the cooled sponges in clingfilm and store in the freezer for up to 3 months. Fill and ice the cake once it has defrosted.

SQUIDGY CHOCOLATE FUDGE CAKE

Everyone loves a chocolate cake. This light sponge, covered in shiny chocolate frosting is superb. You would never know it was gluten-free!

MAKES: ONE 20CM ROUND CAKE
PREPARATION: 20 MINUTES,
PLUS FILLING AND ICING
COOKING: 20–25 MINUTES

For the sponge

vegetable oil, for oiling

225g Gluten-Free Flour Mix B
(see page 22)

1 teaspoon xanthan gum

1 teaspoon baking powder
(see box, page 19)

½ teaspoon bicarbonate of soda

50g cocoa powder

100g unsalted butter, softened

250g dark muscovado sugar

3 medium eggs, beaten,
at room temperature

1 teaspoon vanilla extract

1 teaspoon glycerine

200ml semi-skimmed milk

For the frosting

225g dark chocolate (see box,
page 19), chopped

142ml carton double cream

100g unsalted butter, softened

120g icing sugar, sieved

rose petals, optional

Preheat the oven to 180°C/gas mark 4. Oil two 20cm Victoria sandwich tins and base-line with baking parchment.

Sieve the flour, xanthan gum, baking powder, bicarbonate of soda and cocoa powder together.

In a deep bowl, cream the butter and muscovado sugar together until light and fluffy. Gradually beat in the eggs, vanilla and glycerine. Fold tablespoonfuls of the flour mixture into the butter and egg mix, alternately with the milk, until the batter is evenly combined.

Divide the mixture between the tins and level the surface. Bake on the same shelf in the centre of the oven for about 25 minutes. The cakes are ready when a skewer inserted into the sponge comes out clean.

Leave the cakes to cool in the tins for 10 minutes and then turn out onto a wire rack to cool completely.

For the frosting, melt the chocolate, with the cream, in a heatproof bowl in a microwave, or set over a pan of just simmering water. Stir very gently until the mixture is smooth. Allow to cool to room temperature. Cream the softened butter with the icing sugar and then whisk this into the chocolate mixture until it is the thickness of soft butter.

Put one sponge (top down) onto a serving plate and spread with some of the frosting, leaving a generous amount for the top. Sandwich with the second sponge and spread the rest of the frosting over the top and sides. Chill well in the fridge. Remove from the fridge 15 minutes before eating. Decorate with rose petals, silver leaf or other decoration of your choice.

☐ **TO STORE:** The filled cake will keep for up to 3 days in an airtight container in the fridge.

✳ **TO FREEZE:** Freeze the iced cake, uncovered. Once the icing is solid, cover, wrap well and return to the freezer.

SIMNEL CAKE

This is a golden, rich fruit cake topped with marzipan and traditionally served at Easter. It would also make a wonderful birthday or special-occasion cake.

MAKES: ONE 20CM ROUND CAKE
PREPARATION: 30 MINUTES
COOKING: 1½–1¾ HOURS

---

vegetable oil, for greasing

500g natural-coloured marzipan
(see box, page 19)

225g Gluten-Free Flour Mix B
(see page 22)

1 teaspoon baking powder
(see box, page 19)

1 teaspoon xanthan gum

½ teaspoon ground cinnamon

½ teaspoon ground allspice

½ teaspoon grated nutmeg

225g unsalted butter, softened

225g golden caster sugar

4 medium eggs, at room
temperature

25g ground almonds

2 tablespoons brandy

225g sultanas

125g currants

100g natural-coloured glacé
cherries, halved and washed

grated zest of 1 large lemon

For the top

2 tablespoons apricot jam, warmed

4 tablespoons golden icing sugar

2 teaspoons lemon juice

Preheat the oven to 160°C/gas mark 3. Oil and line the base and sides of a 6cm deep, 20cm round loose-based cake tin with a double layer of baking parchment. Cut an 85g piece off the marzipan and set aside. Cut the remaining marzipan block in half.

Sift the flour, baking powder, xanthan gum and spices together. In another bowl, beat the butter and the sugar together using an electric whisk, until fluffy and light.

Gradually add the eggs and the flour mixture, alternately, to the creamed mixture. Next, stir in the ground almonds. Stir in the brandy and then mix in the dried fruit, cherries and lemon zest and give the whole mixture a really good stir.

Spoon half of the mixture into the tin and level. Roll out one of the larger pieces of marzipan (use the base of the cake tin as a guide) and cut to a circle to fit the tin. Lay this carefully over the cake mixture. Spoon in the other half of the cake mixture, level out and bake for 1½–1¾ hours or until a skewer inserted into the centre comes out clean.

Leave the cake to cool in the tin. When it has cooled completely, take it out of the tin, remove the paper and turn it upside down onto a serving plate, so you have a flat top.

Brush what is now the top of the cake with a little of the warmed apricot jam. Roll out the larger remaining piece of marzipan to fit the top of the cake exactly and press it down flat. Decorate the edge of the marzipan with a 'pinching' effect.

Divide the reserved 85g marzipan into 11 balls. Using the remaining jam, stick the balls around the edge of the cake. Finally, mix a little lemon juice into the icing sugar to give a soft spreading consistency and pour it onto the centre of the cake. Finish with a large ribbon around the side of the cake.

☐ **TO STORE:** Keeps for up to 1 week in an airtight container.

✱ **TO FREEZE:** Wrap the un-iced cake well in clingfilm and foil and freeze in an airtight container. Decorate with the marzipan once defrosted.

RICOTTA CAKE WITH COFFEE SYRUP

A few years ago I worked in northern Italy, where we would have a cake like this with coffee after lunch. The ricotta gives the cake a good texture and flavour and the coffee syrup soaks in really well to finish it off perfectly. This is a great one for Father's Day!

MAKES: ONE 22CM SQUARE CAKE
PREPARATION: 15 MINUTES
COOKING: 35–40 MINUTES

For the cake

vegetable oil, for oiling

125g butter, softened

185g caster sugar

150g ricotta cheese

2 medium eggs, beaten, at room temperature

200g Gluten-Free Flour Mix B (see page 22)

2 teaspoons baking powder (see box, page 19)

1 teaspoon xanthan gum

2 teaspoons instant coffee dissolved in 2 tablespoons boiling water

For the syrup

100ml brandy

100g sugar

4 teaspoons instant coffee

sieved icing sugar, for dusting

Preheat the oven to 180°C/gas mark 4. Oil a 22cm square tin and base-line with baking parchment.

Place the softened butter and sugar in a mixing bowl and beat with a hand-held electric whisk until creamed together. Add the ricotta and eggs and mix well.

Next, sieve the flour, baking powder and xanthan gum together so that they are evenly mixed. Add this to the ricotta mixture and finally stir in the coffee liquid. Mix well.

Spread into the prepared tin and bake for about 35 minutes. The cake is ready when a skewer inserted into the centre comes out clean.

For the syrup, place the brandy, sugar and coffee together into a saucepan and bring to a simmer to dissolve the sugar. Turn the heat down and cook for 2 minutes to thicken. Set aside.

Once the cake is cooked, remove it from the oven, cool slightly in the tin and prick with a skewer all over. Pour over the warm syrup and leave to cool.

Once cooled, remove the cake from the tin and peel off the paper. To serve, cut into squares and dust with icing sugar.

☐ **TO STORE:** The cake will keep for up to 1 week in an airtight container.

✱ **TO FREEZE:** Place the un-dusted cake in an airtight container and freeze. Defrost for 1–2 hours and when defrosted, sprinkle with icing sugar.

BONFIRE PARKIN WITH GINGER ICING

There are different versions of parkin from Lancashire and Yorkshire but this one is adapted from my mum's recipe – she always used to make it on Bonfire night.

MAKES: ONE 28 x 18 x 3CM CAKE
PREPARATION: 15 MINUTES
COOKING: 45 MINUTES

For the parkin

vegetable oil, for oiling

225g Gluten-Free Flour Mix B (see page 22)

1 teaspoon ground ginger

1 teaspoon ground mixed spice

1 teaspoon xanthan gum

225g very fine oatmeal (see box, page 19)

275g black treacle

225g unrefined golden caster sugar

175g unsalted butter, softened

1 teaspoon bicarbonate of soda

125ml semi-skimmed milk

For the ginger icing

150g golden icing sugar, sieved

2 tablespoons ginger syrup (from a jar of preserved stem ginger)

few slivers of preserved stem ginger, chopped

Preheat the oven to 180°C/gas mark 4. Oil and base-line a 28 × 18 × 3cm baking tray.

Sift the flour, ginger, mixed spice and xanthan gum together. Add the oatmeal and stir well. Gently heat the treacle, sugar and butter together in a pan until melted and nice and runny. Dissolve the bicarbonate of soda in the milk. Pour the melted butter mixture into the dry ingredients and then add the milk mixture. Carefully stir together and pour into the prepared baking tray.

Bake for about 45 minutes or until well risen and firm. Allow the parkin to cool in the tin.

To make the icing, sift the icing sugar into a bowl; add the ginger syrup and just enough cold water to mix until smooth and thick. Spread the icing over the cooled cake, decorate with slivers of chopped ginger and then cut into slices.

☐ **TO STORE:** The cake will keep for 2 days stored in an airtight container.

✱ **TO FREEZE:** Wrap the un-iced cake in greaseproof paper and foil, and freeze in an airtight container. Defrost for 1–2 hours and when defrosted, ice and decorate as above.

RICH FRUIT CHRISTMAS CAKE

I actually prefer this gluten-free version of Christmas cake to the regular kind. The texture is just the same if not better and it is delicious! It's best to soak the fruit in the whisky and lemon juice overnight; it makes a real difference to the texture of the cake.

For the cake

75g currants

75g sultanas

350g raisins

50g mixed peel

150ml whisky

grated zest and juice of
   1 small lemon

vegetable oil, for oiling

150g Gluten-Free Flour Mix B
   (see page 22)

1 teaspoon baking powder
   (see box, page 19)

1 teaspoon xanthan gum

1 teaspoon mixed spice

1 teaspoon ground allspice

150g unsalted butter, softened

150g soft dark brown sugar

3 medium eggs, at room
   temperature

50g ground almonds

2 tablespoons semi-skimmed
   milk

50g whole almonds

100g natural-coloured glacé
   cherries, halved and washed

1 tablespoon black treacle

1 tablespoon clear honey

For the top

2 tablespoons smooth apricot
   jam, warmed

100g mixed glacé fruits, e.g.
   red or green cherries, ginger,
   melon or pineapple

50g nuts, e.g. almonds,
   walnuts, pecan halves

MAKES: ONE 18 CM ROUND OR
SQUARE CAKE
PREPARATION: 20 MINUTES,
PLUS OVERNIGHT SOAKING TIME
COOKING: 1½–2 HOURS

Place the dried fruit and mixed peel in a pan, add the whisky and the lemon juice and zest, and bring up to the boil. Take the pan off the heat, cover and leave to soak overnight.

Preheat the oven to 150°C/gas mark 2. Oil and line the base and sides of a 6–8cm deep round or square 18cm cake tin with a double layer of baking parchment, including a tall collar sticking up.

Sift the flour, baking powder, xanthan gum and spices together. Cream the butter and sugar together until fluffy and light. Gradually add the eggs and flour, alternately, and then add the ground almonds. Stir in the milk and mix in the dried fruit mixture, almonds and cherries. Finally stir in the treacle and honey and give the whole cake mix a thoroughly good stir.

Spoon the mixture into the tin, level, and bake for about 1½–2 hours or until a skewer inserted into the centre comes out clean. Leave to cool in the tin.

To decorate, brush the surface of the cake with half the warmed jam. Arrange or pile a selection of glacé fruits and nuts over the top and brush over a second layer of jam to glaze. Now all you need is a big bow to put round the sides!

Fancy a traditional topping?

I like the glacé fruit and nut topping as it's so quick and easy! But if you prefer you can decorate it in the traditional way with a layer of marzipan topped with white icing of your choice.

☐ **TO STORE:** The undecorated cake will keep for up to 1 month, tightly wrapped in foil in an airtight container.

✳ **TO FREEZE:** When cold, remove the cake from the tin, wrap in greaseproof paper and two thick layers of foil and freeze in an airtight container. Defrost for 3–4 hours and when defrosted decorate as above.

CHOCOLATE CHERRY TRIFLE CAKE

MAKES: ONE TALL 20CM CAKE
PREPARATION: 20 MINUTES
COOKING: 12–15 MINUTES

---

vegetable oil, for oiling

2 medium eggs, at room temperature

225g caster sugar

175g Gluten-Free Flour Mix A (see page 22)

pinch of salt

1½ teaspoons baking powder (see box, page 19)

1 teaspoon xanthan gum

20g cocoa powder, sieved

130ml sunflower oil

130ml semi-skimmed milk

2 teaspoons vanilla extract

1 teaspoon glycerine, optional

For the filling

75g packet instant custard (see box, page 19)

300ml boiling water

75g dark chocolate (see box, page 19), finely chopped

75g white chocolate, finely chopped

568ml carton double cream

20g icing sugar

400g can cherries in syrup, drained well

To decorate

3-4 tablespoons chocolate sprinkles (see box, page 19)

This cake is great at Christmas when you want something different from the usual. The glycerine is an optional extra and helps to give the sponge a little more shelf life.

Preheat the oven to 180°C/gas mark 4. Oil two 20cm sandwich tins.

Whisk the eggs and sugar together in a medium bowl for about 1 minute by hand. In a separate bowl mix the flour, salt, baking powder, xanthan gum and cocoa powder together really well. Whisk the oil, milk, vanilla and glycerine together in a jug. Add the dry ingredients to the beaten eggs and sugar, then mix in the wet ingredients.

Divide the mixture between the oiled tins and bake for 12–15 minutes, or until well risen and spongy when pressed lightly in the middle. Leave to cool.

Divide the instant custard equally between two clean bowls, and then pour 150ml boiling water onto each, whisking well. Add the white chocolate to one bowl and the dark chocolate to the other, whisking well to melt the chocolate completely. Then set aside to cool until thickened.

Lightly whip the cream with the icing sugar.

Carefully slice each cooled sponge in half widthways. Place one of sponge layers on a serving plate. Spread some dark chocolate custard onto it, then dot with some cherries and fill in the gaps with a little white chocolate custard and whipped cream. Continue layering the sponges and fillings in this way until you reach the top (make sure you save enough whipped cream for the topping). Press the final sponge down lightly.

Spread whipped cream over the top of the cake, and decorate with some canned or fresh cherries. Scatter with some chocolate sprinkles for that finishing touch.

☐ **TO STORE:** The sponges will keep for 1 day in an airtight container.

✱ **TO FREEZE:** The plain sponges can be frozen. Wrap in foil and freeze in an airtight container. Defrost for 1–2 hours.

TRAYBAKES
& BARS

MARSHMALLOW CRISPIES

Classic kids' stuff here, but I have seen many an adult tuck into these at a kids' party... be warned, they are very moreish!

MAKES: 16
PREPARATION: 10 MINUTES
COOKING: 10 MINUTES

---

vegetable oil, for oiling

50g unsalted butter

200g large marshmallows
(see box, page 19)

150g mixed dried fruit, e.g.
chopped apricots and raisins

50g gluten-free biscuits or
shortbread (try the recipe
on page 23), crumbled

150g gluten-free crisp puffed
rice cereal

75g dark chocolate (see box,
page 19)

Oil a 24cm square baking tin and base-line with baking parchment.

Heat the butter, until melted, in a medium, non-stick pan. Next add the marshmallows and stir over a low heat until completely melted; take care not to burn or boil the mixture. Off the heat, stir in the fruit, the crumbled biscuits and finally add the crisp puffed rice cereal. Mix well.

Press the mixture down lightly into the prepared tin.

Melt the chocolate, in a heatproof bowl, in a microwave, or set over a pan of just simmering water – don't let the bowl touch the water. Drizzle the chocolate over the cake and leave to chill in the fridge until firm.

Cut into 16 oblongs or squares to serve.

☐ **TO STORE:** The crispies will keep for 1 week stored in an airtight container.

✽ **TO FREEZE:** Wrap well and freeze in a plastic bag.

PECAN HONEY FLAPJACKS

I know everybody cooks flapjacks, but this recipe is bulked up with the addition of roasted pecans – an idea I picked up in the States. They really add to the flavour and texture.

MAKES: 10–12
PREPARATION: 10 MINUTES
COOKING: 20 MINUTES

---

vegetable oil, for oiling

100g pecan nut halves, roughly chopped

200g butter

200g dark muscovado sugar

200g clear honey

400g porridge oats (see box, page 19)

100g sesame seeds

170g semi-dried cranberries

2 teaspoons ground allspice

Preheat the oven to 180°C/gas mark 4. Line a baking tray with baking parchment. Oil a 33 × 24 × 3cm deep baking tin and base-line with baking parchment.

Place the pecans on the lined tray, and brown them well in the oven for 8–10 minutes. Once browned, remove from the oven and cool.

Increase the oven temperature to 200°C/gas mark 6.

Heat the butter, until melted, in a medium, non-stick pan. Then add the sugar and honey and mix well until the sugar has dissolved. Add the pecans, oats, sesame seeds, cranberries and allspice and mix really well. Spoon the mixture into the prepared baking tin and press down evenly.

Bake for 20 minutes or until golden; adjust the time according to your oven.

Once cooked, allow the flapjacks to cool in the tin and then cut into 10–12 even pieces.

☐ **TO STORE:** The flapjacks will keep for 1 week in an airtight container.

✳ **TO FREEZE:** Wrap well and store in a plastic bag.

APRICOT & ALMOND MACAROON BARS

These have a lovely chewy texture and make a really tasty treat for a picnic or lunch box.

MAKES: 16
PREPARATION: 20 MINUTES
COOKING: 40–45 MINUTES

For the base

vegetable oil, for oiling

150g rice flour

50g golden caster sugar

25g light muscovado sugar

75g unsalted butter, cubed

4 tablespoons apricot jam

For the filling

225g semi-dried apricots, roughly chopped

1 tablespoon lemon juice

2 medium eggs, at room temperature

1 teaspoon vanilla extract

125g demerara sugar

25g rice flour

½ teaspoon baking powder (see box, page 19)

50g ground almonds

demerara sugar and flaked almonds, for sprinkling

Preheat the oven to 180°C/gas mark 4. Oil a 4cm deep, 22cm square tin and base-line with baking parchment.

Put the flour and sugars for the base into a food processor and blend together. Add the butter and process until the mixture forms fine crumbs and then starts to clump together. Tip the crumb mixture into the base of the prepared tin and press lightly to make an even layer.

Cook the base for 10–15 minutes or until pale golden brown. When cool, brush with the apricot jam.

Meanwhile, put the semi-dried apricots into a small pan with the lemon juice and 5 tablespoons cold water. Stir over a low heat until soft, thick and fairly smooth. Cool slightly, then spread over the base and set aside.

Start whisking the eggs and the vanilla together and then whisk in the sugar until thickened and airy. Stir the flour and baking powder together and fold into the sugar-egg mixture. Lastly, fold in the ground almonds.

Spoon the topping onto the apricot base and sprinkle the demerara sugar and flaked almonds on top. Return the tin to the oven for about 30 minutes, until golden and risen.

Remove from the oven and allow to cool in the tin, then cut into 16 bars.

☐ **TO STORE:** The bars will keep for 1 week stored in an airtight container.

✳ **TO FREEZE:** Wrap well and freeze in an airtight container.

FUDGY COFFEE MACADAMIA CRUNCH

This is a really tasty sweet treat, but take care not to overwhisk the egg whites or the texture will end up slightly firmer than desired. I like to add alternate spoonfuls of the two mixtures to the tin to give a nice marbled effect.

Any nuts will do for the praline topping, or you can just use the sugar on its own.

MAKES: 9 SQUARES
PREPARATION: 25 MINUTES
COOKING: 30 MINUTES

For the sponge base

vegetable oil, for oiling

175g unsalted butter

5 large eggs, separated,
  at room temperature

200g soft light brown sugar

200g ground almonds (see
  Cook's note, below)

1 teaspoon xanthan gum

2 tablespoons instant coffee
  dissolved in 1 tablespoon
  boiling water

For the praline topping

100g caster sugar

100g macadamia nuts

Cook's note

For the sponge base, I like to
use whole blanched almonds
and grind them myself, either
in a food processor or by
bashing them in a sealed bag
with a rolling pin. This gives
a slightly different texture and
I think it tastes even better.

Preheat the oven to 180°C/gas mark 4. Oil a 4cm deep, 22cm square baking tin and base-line with baking parchment. Oil or line a baking sheet with baking parchment for the praline.

Melt the butter in a small pan. Stir the egg yolks into the sugar in a large mixing bowl and then gradually add the melted butter.

Whisk the egg whites until they form soft peaks. Fold the whites into the yolk mixture very lightly, so you don't lose all the air, and then add the ground almonds and the xanthan gum, very gently. Put half the mixture into a separate bowl and mix the liquid coffee into that portion.

Spoon some of each mixture alternately into the prepared tin and repeat to create layers; drag a spoon back and forth a couple of times to create a marbled mixture.

Bake in the centre of the oven for about 30 minutes. The top will be firm and the centre still a bit soft. Stand the tin on a wire rack and leave to cool completely.

To make the praline topping, place the sugar and macadamia nuts together in a large frying pan over a low heat. Keep watching; swirl the pan occasionally, until all the sugar has completely dissolved to a rich brown liquid (about 10 minutes). You may have to stir the last of the sugar crystals in and keep an eye on the pan, because it burns easily.

Pour this mixture on to the prepared baking sheet, spreading the macadamia nuts out in a single layer. Leave the mixture to cool and become brittle, then lift it off the baking tray into a double-layered strong freezer bag. Break it up with a few bashes from a rolling pin and then crush it quite finely, with the rolling pin.

Remove the cake from the tin and peel off the paper. Turn it right side up and place on a board, then spoon the praline on top of the cake and cut into squares.

☐ **TO STORE:** The bars will keep for 1 week stored in an airtight container.

✳ **TO FREEZE:** Cool the sponge, wrap well and freeze, without the topping. Add the crunch topping after defrosting.

CHOCOLATE CARAMEL ROCKY ROAD SHORTBREAD

I just had to put this in the book! It is fast becoming a real classic; everywhere you go these days rocky road is on the menu. Cut into thick squares is the only way here.

MAKES: 12 LARGE SQUARES
PREPARATION: 15 MINUTES
PLUS CHILLING AND SETTING
COOKING: 15–20 MINUTES

For the base

vegetable oil, for oiling

100g cornflour

100g rice flour

50g golden caster sugar

30g light muscovado sugar

120g unsalted butter, cubed

For the filling

150g butter

150g soft light brown sugar

405g can condensed milk

For the topping

150g dark chocolate (see box, page 19)

25g chopped pecan or brazil nuts

50g white chocolate buttons (see box, page 19), chopped

25g dried cranberries

20g mini marshmallows (see box, page 19)

Preheat the oven to 190°C/gas mark 5. Lightly oil a 6cm deep, 20cm square tin and line the base and sides with baking parchment.

Put the flours and sugars for the base into a food processor and blend together. Add the butter and pulse until the mixture starts to clump together. Tip the crumb mixture into the base of the prepared tin and press very lightly to make an even layer. Bake the base in the oven for about 15 minutes or until pale golden brown.

To make the filling, place the butter and the sugar in a large non-stick pan over a low heat, stirring until the butter melts and the sugar dissolves. Add the condensed milk and bring gently to the boil, stirring continuously. Bubble gently for just 2 minutes, then remove from the heat. Spoon the caramel over the cooked base, covering to the edges, and leave to cool for 30 minutes.

For the topping, melt the chocolate in a heatproof bowl set over a pan of just simmering water – don't let the bowl touch the water. Alternatively you could use a microwave to gently melt the chocolate. Mix the remaining topping ingredients into the melted chocolate and stir well. Spoon the mixture evenly over the caramel base. Leave to set in the fridge and then cut it into squares, to serve.

☐ **TO STORE:** The shortbread will keep for 1 week stored in an airtight container.

✱ **TO FREEZE:** Wrap well and freeze in an airtight container.

STICKY DATE, RUM & CARAMEL CAKE

A nice squidgy caramel cake based on the sticky toffee pudding recipe. I serve mine with ice cream or thick double cream. Medjool dates are best for this recipe, as they have a wonderful, melting, gooey texture.

MAKES: 6–8 SQUARES
PREPARATION: 10 MINUTES
COOKING: 20 MINUTES

vegetable oil, for oiling

175g soft dates, stoned and
   roughly chopped

1 teaspoon bicarbonate
   of soda

5 tablespoons dark rum
   or brandy

100ml boiling water

175g Gluten-Free Flour Mix B
   (see page 22)

1 teaspoon xanthan gum

1 teaspoon baking powder
   (see box, page 19)

75g unsalted butter, softened

150g dark muscovado sugar

2 medium eggs, beaten,
   at room temperature

For the toffee sauce

400g dulce de leche, from
   a jar or tin

Preheat the oven to 180°C/gas mark 4. Oil an 18cm square baking tin and base-line with baking parchment.

Put the dates, bicarbonate of soda, rum and boiling water into a small, heatproof bowl. Microwave on full power for 1 minute and set aside to cool.

Sieve the flour, xanthan gum and baking powder together. Using a hand-held electric whisk, cream the butter with the sugar until it is light and fluffy and then gradually beat in the eggs. Fold in tablespoonfuls of the flour mixture, with alternate spoonfuls of the soaked dates and the liquid, until the batter is evenly combined.

Pour the mixture into the prepared tin and level the surface. Bake in the centre of the oven for about 20 minutes, until firm and springy and a skewer inserted into the centre comes out clean.

To serve, spread the warm sponge with a layer of dulce de leche and cut into squares.

☐ **TO STORE:** The sponge cake will keep for 1 week (without the topping) stored in an airtight container. Top with the dulce de leche when you are ready to serve.

✳ **TO FREEZE:** Wrap well and freeze in an airtight container. Defrost, warm for 10–15 seconds in the microwave and finish with the dulce de leche when you are ready to serve.

BREAD

CRISPY TORTILLA CHIPS

I love these! They are better than any on the market, completely gluten-free and really easy to make. It is best to cook them in small batches.

MAKES: ABOUT 20
PREPARATION: 10 MINUTES
COOKING: 10 MINUTES

100g Gluten-Free Flour Mix A (see page 22)

50g fine polenta (see box, page 19)

¾ teaspoon xanthan gum

½ teaspoon baking powder (see box, page 19)

2 pinches of salt

about 130ml warm water

cornflour, for dusting

vegetable oil, for deep frying

salt and chilli powder, for dusting

Place the flour, polenta, xanthan gum, baking powder and salt in a bowl. Add enough warm water to form a soft dough.

Remove from the bowl and knead well for 2–3 minutes, using a little dusting of cornflour to stop the dough sticking to the work surface.

Divide the dough into 6–8 pieces – the smaller the pieces of dough, the easier it is to roll them out.

Dust a rolling pin well with cornflour and roll out a piece of dough as thinly as possible. Cut into small triangles.

Heat the vegetable oil to about 175–180°C (check the temperature using a thermometer or drop in a piece of bread – when it turns golden brown in 30 seconds the oil is ready) and deep fry the tortillas in small batches until crisp on both sides.

Drain well on kitchen paper, and dust with salt and chilli powder to serve.

☐ **TO STORE:** The chips will keep for up to 2 days stored in an airtight container.

✳ **TO FREEZE:** Not suitable.

INDIAN-STYLE FLATBREADS

The Indians make great flatbreads. Here is a twist on the basic flatbread principle, delicious with all sorts of food and great for dipping. I find it's best to leave them to cool completely to crisp up, then reheat them on a hot griddle or in a non-stick frying pan for 30 seconds, before eating.

MAKES: 6 BREADS
PREPARATION: 10 MINUTES
COOKING: 3–4 MINUTES FOR EACH BREAD

150g Gluten-Free Flour Mix A (see page 22)

½ teaspoon xanthan gum

3–4 pinches of salt (optional)

½ teaspoon whole cumin seeds

¼ teaspoon freshly ground black pepper

½ teaspoon baking powder (see box, page 19)

4 tablespoons olive oil

about 120ml warm water

cornflour, for dusting

olive oil, for brushing

Place the flour, xanthan gum, salt, cumin seeds, pepper and baking powder in a bowl and mix well. Add the oil and three-quarters of the warm water and mix to form a wet dough. You may need to add a little more water to achieve this – aim for a slightly loose mix. Knead well on a board, using a little cornflour to stop the dough sticking.

Cut the dough into 6 equal pieces. Roll out each piece into a circle, approximately 15cm in diameter, as thin as you can – the thinner the better. Brush half of each circle with olive oil, then carefully fold in half and press together to form a semi-circle.

Heat a griddle pan or a 23cm non-stick frying pan over a medium-high heat, then place the first bread straight in the pan, with no oil. Cook for 2–3 minutes on each side, until the bread is slightly scorched on both sides. Remove from the pan, place on a wire rack and brush lightly with olive oil. Repeat the process until all the breads are cooked and serve straight away.

☐ **TO STORE:** These are best served straight away and I don't recommend storing them.

✱ **TO FREEZE:** Not suitable.

POPPY SEED BREADSTICKS

Easy to make and surprisingly moreish – good with dips and soups. Sesame seeds, caraway seeds and fennel seeds also work well. You can make these by hand or in a breadmaker.

MAKES: 20
PREPARATION: 30 MINUTES,
PROVING TIME: 1 HOUR
COOKING: 10–15 MINUTES

325g Gluten-Free Bread Mix
　(see page 22)

2 teaspoons xanthan gum

1 teaspoon salt

2 teaspoons caster sugar

7g sachet easy-blend
　dried yeast

1 small egg, at room
　temperature

225ml warm water

2 tablespoons olive oil

cornflour, for dusting

vegetable oil, for oiling

1 egg, beaten, for brushing

1 tablespoon poppy seeds

If you are making the dough by hand, put the flour, xanthan gum, salt, sugar and yeast into a large bowl, mix thoroughly and make a well in the centre. Stir the egg, water and oil together in a jug and pour into the flour. Mix with a wooden spoon and when the mixture tightens to form a dough turn it out onto a board, dusted with cornflour. Flour your hands with cornflour and knead the dough for 5–10 minutes until smooth.

Place the dough in a clean bowl, cover with oiled clingfilm and set it aside in a warm place to prove for about an hour, until doubled and puffy: how long will depend on how warm it is.

If you have a breadmaker it's easier to control the variables and achieve a more consistent result. Simply pour the water, egg and oil mixture into the pan first; add the flour mixture next and sprinkle the yeast on top last. Set the machine to 'dough' and leave it to do the kneading and the proving.

Preheat the oven to 220°C/gas mark 7. Oil two baking sheets. Prepare your work surface with a large sheet of baking parchment dusted with cornflour.

Turn out the dough and pat it into a rough rectangle about 25 × 15 × 1cm thick. Cut it in half across and then into equal strips, like fingers. Handle the dough gently and roll each strip with the palm of your hand into a long stick. (The thinner the sticks, the drier the texture.)

Transfer the breadsticks to a plate, brush with the beaten egg, and sprinkle with poppy seeds. Repeat for all the breadsticks, carefully lifting them onto the oiled baking sheet. Cover the line of breadsticks with oiled clingfilm as you do this, and they will rise slightly at room temperature.

Bake the breadsticks for 10–15 minutes until crisp and puffed. Allow to cool on the baking trays.

These are best eaten fresh-baked, but you can refresh them in the microwave for a few seconds before serving.

☐ **TO STORE:** The breadsticks, if dried out well, will keep for up to 1 week in an airtight container.

✴ **TO FREEZE:** Freeze when cool, well wrapped and stored in an airtight container.

PARMESAN, SAGE & ROAST GARLIC SCONES

I like savoury scones, especially when spread with cold salted butter. I like them topped with guacamole, houmous or even crab or prawn cocktail.

MAKES: 10–12
PREPARATION: 10 MINUTES
COOKING: 30–35 MINUTES

---

vegetable oil, for oiling

6 cloves garlic, unpeeled

300g Gluten-Free Flour Mix A
   (see page 22)

75g cooking margarine

pinch of salt

2 teaspoons xanthan gum

3 teaspoons baking powder
   (see box, page 19)

2 medium eggs, beaten,
   at room temperature

2 teaspoons dried sage

50g Parmesan cheese,
   finely grated

125ml semi-skimmed milk,
   warmed

cornflour, for dusting

semi-skimmed milk,
   for brushing

Preheat the oven to 200°C/gas mark 6.

First, roast the garlic: wrap it in foil and bake for 20 minutes. Remove the skins and crush the creamy garlic.

Reduce the oven temperature to 180°C/gas mark 4. Oil two baking trays.

Place the flour, margarine, salt and xanthan gum in a bowl and rub together until you have the consistency of fine breadcrumbs. Add the baking powder, eggs, sage, cheese, milk and roasted garlic paste and mix together to form a dough.

Dust a work surface with cornflour and gently roll the dough out to about 2–3cm thick. Using a 5cm plain cutter, cut out 10–12 scones. Place on the baking trays, brush with milk and bake for 10–15 minutes.

Once cooked, remove from the oven and cool on a wire rack. Cut in half and spread with salted butter to serve.

☐ **TO STORE:** The scones will keep for 2–3 days stored in an airtight container. They will dry out slightly after storing, so sprinkle over a little water and then warm them through in a preheated oven at 200°C/gas mark 6 for 5 minutes before serving.

✳ **TO FREEZE:** Wrap well and freeze in an airtight container. The scones will dry out slightly after freezing, so once thawed, sprinkle over a little water and then warm them through in a preheated oven at 200°C/gas mark 6 for 5 minutes before serving.

FOCCACIA

This recipe took seven attempts to get right – I wanted to achieve a light and spongy texture and good flavour. As you will see, there is no salt in the mix, I find this tends to weaken the protein structure, giving you less of a risen bread. I tend to stick to adding granular rock or sea salt to the top of the bread along with olive oil, rosemary and garlic cloves. I like to include vitamin C powder in this recipe, as I've found it really helps improve the structure of the bread. It is widely available from chemists.

MAKES: ONE 30CM BREAD
PREPARATION: 20 MINUTES
COOKING: 15–20 MINUTES

---

vegetable oil, for greasing

2 x 7g sachets easy-blend
    dried yeast

500ml warm water

2 teaspoons caster sugar

500g Gluten-Free Bread Mix
    (see page 22)

1 teaspoon xanthan gum

2 teaspoons baking powder
    (see box, page 19)

1 teaspoon vitamin C powder

2 egg whites

10 garlic cloves, halved

4 tablespoons olive oil

1 tablespoon sea salt

4–6 sprigs fresh rosemary

Oil a 3.5cm deep 30cm non-stick pizza pan.

Whisk the yeast, water and sugar together well, then cover and leave in a warm place for 15 minutes to activate.

Meanwhile, place the flour, xanthan gum, baking powder and vitamin C powder into a bowl and mix well.

When the yeast is frothy, whisk the egg whites until foamy. Pour the yeast mixture over the flour and add the whisked egg white and bring together. Mix well, but do not over-mix.

Spoon into the oiled pizza tray, cover lightly with clingfilm and press down lightly with your hands. Remove the clingfilm.

Press the halved garlic cloves into the dough and re-cover with a fresh piece of clingfilm. Leave to prove in a warm place for 15–20 minutes, or until just doubled in height.

Meanwhile, preheat the oven to 220°C/gas mark 7.

Once the dough has risen, carefully remove the clingfilm, spoon over the oil and sprinkle over the salt and rosemary. Bake for 15 minutes or until well browned.

Remove from the oven and cool on a wire rack. Slice into wedges to serve.

☐ **TO STORE:** The bread will keep for 1 day in an airtight container.

✳ **TO FREEZE:** Once cooled, wrap the bread well and freeze.

PECAN & TREACLE BREAD

In *Seriously Good! Gluten-Free Cooking* I did only one recipe for bread, which contained chestnut flour. The people whose e-mails and letters I received loved it, but many of them had real trouble getting hold of chestnut flour. Not many shops stocked it, and online stores had sporadic supplies and it was quite expensive.

So, here is another bread recipe; the texture is fairly light and airy, with a malt loaf background flavour which comes from the black treacle. It makes great toast.

MAKES: ONE 25 x 12.5 x 6.5CM LOAF
PREPARATION: 20 MINUTES
COOKING: 20–25 MINUTES

---

vegetable oil, for oiling

2 x 7g sachets easy-blend dried yeast

450–500ml warm water

2 teaspoons sugar

400g Gluten-Free Bread Mix (see page 22)

1 teaspoon salt

50g pecan nuts, roughly chopped

2 teaspoons baking powder (see box, page 19)

2 teaspoons xanthan gum

1 tablespoon black treacle

50g cooking margarine

1 medium egg, beaten

Oil a 25 × 12.5 × 6.5cm loaf tin.

Whisk the yeast, water and sugar together well, then cover and leave in a warm place for 15 minutes to activate.

Meanwhile, place the flour, salt, nuts, baking powder and xanthan gum together in a large bowl and mix well. Place the treacle and margarine in a small non-stick pan and warm through gently until the margarine has melted. Remove from the heat and stir in the egg.

When the yeast mixture is ready, pour it over the flour mixture and add the treacle mixture. Mix well with a wooden spoon, but do not go mad, or the mixture will tighten considerably.

Spoon the mixture into the oiled loaf tin, cover with clingfilm and press the mixture into the tin, then lift off the clingfilm. Cover lightly with a clean piece of clingfilm and leave to prove in a warm place for 20 minutes.

Meanwhile, preheat the oven to 220°C/gas mark 7.

Once the dough is well risen, bake the loaf for 20 minutes until well risen and nicely coloured. Remove from the tin and cool on a wire rack.

☐ **TO STORE:** Once cooled, wrap well in clingfilm or store in an airtight container for up to 3 days.

✱ **TO FREEZE:** Wrap well and freeze in an airtight container. Defrost to room temperature before eating.

RUM-SOAKED BABAS WITH APRICOT GLAZE

Babas are yeasty fruit buns soaked in rum syrup and used to be all the rage at dinner parties. Serve with vanilla ice cream or for a real treat, my favourite – clotted cream.

MAKES: 12
PREPARATION: 30 MINUTES
PROVING TIME: 45 MINUTES
COOKING: 15–20 MINUTES

For the babas

vegetable oil, for oiling

150ml warm water

2 x 7g sachets easy-blend dried yeast

75g caster sugar

200g Gluten-Free Flour Mix B (see page 22)

1 teaspoon xanthan gum

2 teaspoons baking powder (see box, page 19)

100g sultanas

50g currants

50g cooking margarine

1 teaspoon glycerine

2 teaspoons vanilla extract

3 medium egg whites, at room temperature

cornflour, for dusting

For the syrup

225g caster sugar

4–6 tablespoons rum

6 tablespoons apricot jam

Generously oil a 12-hole non-stick muffin tin.

Mix the warm water, yeast and 2 teaspoons of the caster sugar. Whisk well, cover with clingfilm and set aside.

In a separate bowl place the flour, xanthan gum, baking powder, remaining sugar and fruit and mix really well.

Melt the margarine in a small non-stick pan and add the glycerine and vanilla to the pan.

Whisk the egg whites until foamy, but not too stiff.

Pour the yeast mixture over the flour and fruit, then add the melted margarine mixture and finally the egg whites. Fold together well, but do not go mad.

Spoon the mixture into the prepared muffin tins, press down lightly with fingers dusted with cornflour, and cover with clingfilm. Leave the tray in a warm place to rise to the top of the tins (about 45 minutes in a warm airing cupboard).

When proved, preheat the oven to 200°C/gas mark 6. Cook the babas for 10–15 minutes, until well risen and lightly coloured. Remove from the oven and cool in the tin for 5–10 minutes.

Make the syrup by placing the sugar, rum and 225ml cold water in a small pan and simmering until the sugar has dissolved. Once dissolved, place the babas in one by one and turn over several times so they soak up the hot syrup. Once well soaked, carefully lift out with a spatula and place on a wire rack to drain well and cool.

Heat the apricot jam and 1 tablespoon water until well mixed and then, using a pastry brush, coat the babas thoroughly with the glaze and allow to cool again.

☐ **TO STORE:** The babas will keep for up to 2 days, before soaking and glazing, stored in an airtight container. Soak and glaze as above before serving.

✳ **TO FREEZE:** Wrap well when cool and freeze, before soaking and glazing. Defrost for 1 hour, then soak and glaze.

SULTANA BRIOCHE LOAF

One of the nicest breads to eat, especially for breakfast. This recipe goes very close to the real thing, with a lovely flavour and texture.

MAKES: ONE 23 x 13 x 7CM LOAF
PREPARATION: 15 MINUTES
PROVING TIME: 1 HOUR OR SO
IN A WARM PLACE
COOKING: 25–30 MINUTES

---

vegetable oil, for oiling

125ml semi-skimmed milk

1 large egg, at room
    temperature

325g Gluten-Free Flour Mix A
    (see page 22)

1 teaspoon xanthan gum

1 teaspoon salt

25g caster sugar

7g sachet easy-blend
    dried yeast

200g unsalted butter,
    chilled and cubed

75g sultanas

Lightly oil a 23 × 13 × 7cm loaf tin.

In a small pan, warm the milk with 75ml water, add the egg and beat lightly.

Put the flour, xanthan gum, salt, sugar and yeast in a food processor and pulse to mix. Add the butter and process briefly to cut the butter into the mixture. Leave the butter in very small pieces; you don't want it to go to breadcrumbs.

Empty the contents of the food processor into a large bowl. Make a well in the centre and add the sultanas, and the milk and egg liquid. Fold the ingredients together briefly; it will still be a bit lumpy.

Spoon the mixture into the prepared tin. Cover with clingfilm and pat down to flatten nicely, then lift off the film and cover with a fresh piece of clingfilm.

Prove in a warm place for 1 hour.

When proved, preheat the oven to 200°C/gas mark 6. Cook for 25–30 minutes, or until well risen and dark golden. Remove and eat while warm and fresh.

☐ **TO STORE:** The brioche will keep for up to 2 days, stored in an airtight container.

✴ **TO FREEZE:** Slice when cold, double wrap in clingfilm and freeze in an airtight container. Remove individual slices of the bread and toast from frozen as required.

WELSH CAKES

The original base recipe for these cakes came from my step-children's grandmother, Joan. The cakes are so good, and really simple to make; in fact I still have the original recipe she gave me some 10 years ago.

The gluten-free version cakes have a slightly more crumbly texture than usual, but I think it works fine this way. If you like, replace half the margarine with lard – this adds a deeper flavour and also makes a shorter texture.

MAKES: ABOUT 10–12
PREPARATION: 10 MINUTES
COOKING: 15–20 MINUTES

225g Gluten-Free Flour Mix A
  (see page 22)

1 teaspoon mixed spice

100g cooking margarine

½ teaspoon xanthan gum

½ teaspoon bicarbonate of soda

1 teaspoon glycerine

80g caster sugar

80g sultanas

1 medium egg, beaten

cornflour, for dusting

caster sugar, for sprinkling

Place the flour, spice, margarine, xanthan gum and bicarbonate of soda in a bowl and rub through gently with your fingers until you have the texture of fine breadcrumbs. Next add the glycerine, sugar, sultanas and egg and mix together lightly until a soft dough is formed.

Roll the dough out on a work surface dusted with cornflour to a thickness of 5mm. Using a 7cm plain cutter, cut out 10–12 little cakes.

Heat a griddle pan or 23cm non-stick frying pan over a medium heat. Add 4 cakes to the pan and cook for 2–3 minutes on each side, until lightly coloured and puffed.

Once cooked, remove from the pan and sprinkle with caster sugar. Serve warm, spread with butter.

☐ **TO STORE:** The cakes will keep for 2 days stored in an airtight container. Warm through for 10 seconds in the microwave before serving.

✱ **TO FREEZE:** Once cooked, freeze in an airtight container. Defrost for 1 hour and warm through for 10 seconds in the microwave before serving.

CHRISTMAS CHESTNUT & CRANBERRY TEALOAF

This makes a great alternative if you are not too keen on Christmas cake. Chestnut purée really helps the texture of the end result here. And you can get ahead, as it freezes really well.

Serve it spread generously with butter – brandy butter is especially appropriate at Christmas!

MAKES: ONE 23 x 13 x 7CM LOAF
PREPARATION: 15 MINUTES
COOKING: 50–60 MINUTES

vegetable oil, for oiling

125g potato flour

100g tapioca flour

½ teaspoon ground nutmeg

½ teaspoon ground cinnamon

2 teaspoons baking powder
   (see box, page 19)

1 teaspoon xanthan gum

225g unsweetened
   chestnut purée

3 medium eggs, at room
   temperature

100g cooking margarine

150g golden caster sugar

100g dried cranberries

1 tablespoon demerara sugar

Preheat the oven to 170°C/gas mark 3. Oil and base-line a 23 × 13 × 7cm loaf tin.

Sieve the flours together into a medium bowl with the spices, baking powder and xanthan gum.

In a food processor, beat the chestnut purée, then add the eggs one at a time until smooth.

Cream the margarine and sugar together in a large bowl, using a hand-held electric whisk, then add the chestnut mixture; don't worry if it curdles. Next fold in the flour mixture with a large metal spoon, and lastly, stir the cranberries in.

Spoon the mixture into the prepared tin and sprinkle with the demerara sugar. Bake in the centre of the oven for about 50 minutes, or until the top is golden brown and a skewer inserted into the centre comes out clean. Leave to cool in the tin for 10 minutes and then turn out onto a wire rack.

Serve fresh, sliced and buttered.

☐ **TO STORE:** The tealoaf will keep for up to 2 days, stored in an airtight container.

✱ **TO FREEZE:** Cool and slice, then wrap well in clingfilm and freeze. Remove slices of the tealoaf as required, defrost for 1 hour and serve with butter.

PUDDINGS & SWEET TREATS

CHEAT'S RASPBERRY CRÈME BRÛLÉE

This is a recipe from a friend of mine, Paul. He serves it in his pub and it always goes down incredibly well! It is really easy and takes out all the hassle involved in the traditional method. Use clear ramekins if possible so you can see the raspberries inside.

SERVES: 6
PREPARATION: 15 MINUTES

200g ready-made custard
  (see box, page 19)

125g mascarpone cheese

125g crème fraîche

25g caster sugar

300g fresh or frozen
  raspberries

3 tablespoons caster sugar,
  for glazing

Put the custard, mascarpone cheese, crème fraîche and 25g caster sugar into a large bowl and gently whisk together, until the mixture thickens. Divide the raspberries equally between 6 small ramekins (approximately 125ml) and then carefully spoon the creamy mixture over the fruit. Tap the dishes on the worktop so the creamy mixture covers the raspberries, and chill well in the fridge, for about 2 hours.

When you are ready to serve, unless you have a cooks' blow torch, preheat the grill to high. To finish, carefully sprinkle ½ tablespoon caster sugar over each one and place briefly under the hot grill to caramelise or glaze the tops with the blow torch. Serve immediately.

☐ **TO STORE:** Store in the fridge for 2–3 hours if needed before glazing the tops.

✱ **TO FREEZE:** Not suitable.

STRAWBERRY TART WITH CRUSHED MERINGUE & MINT

This is a great summer treat, and any combination of fresh seasonal fruit will work well. Just pile high, top with crushed meringue and drizzle over the yogurt dressing. For best results remove from the fridge 30 minutes before eating, so the fruit is not too cold.

MAKES: ONE 20CM TART
PREPARATION: 10 MINUTES, PLUS CHILLING
COOKING: 25 MINUTES FOR THE PASTRY CASE

For the pastry case

vegetable oil, for oiling

225g Gluten-Free Flour Mix A (see page 22)

1 teaspoon xanthan gum

1 tablespoon caster sugar

100g cooking margarine

1 large egg, at room temperature

cornflour, for dusting

For the filling

250g ready-made custard (see box, page 19)

200g mascarpone cheese

150g strawberries, halved

100g blueberries

1 tablespoon chopped fresh mint

50g meringues (see box, page 19), crushed into large pieces

For the yogurt dressing

200g natural yogurt

4 tablespoons dark maple syrup

2 tablespoons chopped mint

Preheat the oven to 180°C/gas mark 4. Oil a 6cm deep, 20cm loose–based fluted flan tin and base-line with baking parchment.

Mix the flour with the xanthan gum and sugar and then add the margarine, rubbing in until your mixture looks like fine breadcrumbs. Beat the egg, reserve a little to brush the pastry case with during baking, then add the rest of it to your mixture, along with 1 tablespoon water, and mix well to make a dough. Keep an eye on the texture; you may need to add another tablespoon of water so it's nice and soft.

Roll out the pastry, on a work surface dusted with cornflour, to a 22cm circle. Lift the pastry carefully into the tin and press it into the base and up the sides. Shape the pastry into the sides with your thumbs, but don't make it too thin. Line with a layer of baking parchment and baking beans and then bake blind for 15 minutes. Carefully lift out the parchment with the baking beans, brush the pastry case, base and sides, with the remaining beaten egg and return it to the oven for another 10 minutes. Remove and set aside to cool.

Make the filling: beat the custard and mascarpone together in a medium bowl, using a hand-held electric whisk. Spread this mixture into the cooked and cooled pastry case. Top with the strawberries and blueberries. Mix the mint into the crushed meringues and pile on the top. Chill the tart for 30 minutes.

Combine all the dressing ingredients in a serving jug and chill.

Serve the tart no longer than 2 hours after filling it or it will go soggy. Serve chilled slices of the tart with the dressing.

☐ **TO STORE:** The unfilled pastry case can be stored for up to 24 hours in an airtight container.

✱ **TO FREEZE:** Not suitable.

MY MUM'S ORANGE JELLY, PEACH & WHITE CHOCOLATE CHEESECAKE

I have to hold my hand up here; yes this is my mum's recipe – she has been making it for years. It's so simple and the end result is very good indeed, so I just had to steal the recipe!

MAKES: ONE 18CM ROUND CHEESECAKE
PREPARATION: 20 MINUTES, PLUS CHILLING

For the cheesecake

vegetable oil, for oiling

225g gluten-free biscuits or shortbread (try the recipe on page 23)

50g white chocolate (see box, page 19)

135g pack orange jelly

3 tablespoons boiling water

410g can peaches, drained

225g cottage cheese

300ml double cream

For the top

2 fresh peaches, sliced

50g white chocolate (see box, page 19), grated

Oil a 6cm deep, 18cm round, loose-based, non-stick cake tin and base-line with baking parchment.

Place the shortbread in a food processor and process to crumbs. Melt the chocolate, in a heatproof bowl, in the microwave or over a pan of simmering water – don't let the bowl touch the water. Add the melted chocolate to the crumbs and blitz again until the mixture starts to clump together. Press the crumb mixture into the cake tin, without packing it down too much, and then chill really well.

Next, break the jelly into cubes and mix with the boiling water, then melt completely either in a microwave or in a small saucepan. Set aside to cool.

Liquidise the drained peaches until you have a thick purée, then add the cottage cheese, double cream and cooled jelly mix. Liquidise until smooth – probably 15 seconds at the most.

Pour the topping over the base and return to the fridge for at least 1 hour to set.

When set, remove from the fridge and top with the fresh, sliced peaches. Grate the white chocolate over. The cheesecake should be served within 2–3 hours of adding the topping.

☐ **TO STORE:** The cheesecake base can be stored for up to 24 hours in an airtight container, in the fridge.

✱ **TO FREEZE:** Not suitable.

TOFFEE APPLE CRUMBLE

I love toffee apples and this is a great way to include their delicious flavour in a pudding! Bramleys really are the best cooking apple by far – I love their unique, tart flavour, and coupled with toffee, they make a great combination. I like to serve this with ice cream or custard.

SERVES: 4–6
PREPARATION: 15 MINUTES
COOKING: 25–30 MINUTES

175g granulated sugar

100ml cold water

zest and juice of 2 large lemons

3 Bramley apples, peeled, cored and roughly chopped

300g Gluten-Free Flour Mix A (see page 22)

150g unsalted butter, chilled

80g caster sugar

Preheat the oven to 200°C/gas mark 6.

Place the sugar and water in a large saucepan over a high heat and bring to the boil. The sugar will start to thicken over a few minutes and turn slightly brown. Keep an eye on it as it will turn a dark caramel fairly quickly.

Add the lemon zest and juice and the apples to the pan, and cook for 5–6 minutes. Place in a 3cm deep, 24cm square baking dish.

Place the flour and butter in a food processor and blitz until smooth. Just pulse in the sugar, do not overwork. Carefully spoon the topping over the cooked apples.

Bake for 25–30 minutes, or until well browned and cooked. Serve warm.

☐ **TO STORE:** Not suitable.

✱ **TO FREEZE:** Not suitable.

CHOCOLATE CHEESECAKE

No baking book could be without a baked cheesecake – it is just the thing to satisfy a sweet tooth. Just remember not to overcook it – keep it nice and wobbly to ensure a soft melting centre.

MAKES: ONE 18CM ROUND CHEESECAKE
PREPARATION: 15 MINUTES, PLUS OVERNIGHT CHILLING
COOKING: 20 MINUTES, PLUS 1 HOUR SETTING

For the base

vegetable oil, for oiling

125g rice flour

25g golden caster sugar

25g light muscovado or soft light brown sugar

75g unsalted butter, cubed

For the filling

100g dark chocolate (see box, page 19)

400g light or medium-fat cream cheese

100g golden caster sugar

1 teaspoon vanilla extract

200g Greek yogurt

2 medium eggs, at room temperature

For the topping

100g frozen fruits of the forest, defrosted and drained

2 tablespoons cherry jam

Preheat the oven to 180°C/gas mark 4, and set a shelf just below the centre of the oven. Lightly oil a 6cm deep, 18cm loose-based cake tin and base-line with baking parchment.

Put the flour and sugars for the base into a food processor and blend together. Add the butter and process until the mixture forms fine crumbs and then starts to clump together. Tip the crumb mixture into the base of the prepared tin and press lightly to make an even layer. Pop the base into the oven for about 15 minutes or until cooked and pale golden brown. Remove the tin and stand it in a roasting tray.

To make the filling, melt the chocolate, in a heatproof bowl, in the microwave or over a pan of simmering water and set aside. In a large bowl, beat the cream cheese, sugar and vanilla with a hand-held electric mixer and then add the yogurt and the eggs, one at a time. Mix until well blended, then pour the melted chocolate into the bowl and mix until smooth. Pour the filling over the base in the tin and shake gently, to level.

Bake for 20 minutes: it will have just set around the edges but still be wobbly in the middle. Turn the oven off and leave the cheesecake in there to cool slowly for 1 hour; it will continue to cook – and this helps to avoid the top cracking – so don't open the oven door.

Refrigerate until ready to serve, preferably overnight.

To serve, loosen the edges of the cheesecake with a spatula and unmould onto a plate. Crush the fruits lightly, combine with the jam and spoon on top.

☐ **TO STORE:** The cheesecake will keep for up to 2 days, in an airtight container, in the fridge.

✱ **TO FREEZE:** Freeze, uncovered, without the fruit topping. Once frozen, wrap well in clingfilm and foil and return to the freezer. Top with the fruit once defrosted.

HOT CHOCOLATE FONDANT PUDDINGS WITH RASPBERRIES

This is a classic, simple pudding that never fails to impress. The individual puds can be made up to 24 hours in advance, stored in the fridge, and then baked when you are ready. Remember, don't overcook them, and serve with lashings of cream or ice cream.

I like to use semi-thawed frozen raspberries for these puds, as they produce more delicious juice than fresh berries.

SERVES: 6
PREPARATION: 20 MINUTES
COOKING: 12–15 MINUTES

---

vegetable oil, for oiling

350g dark chocolate
   (see box, page 19)

50g unsalted butter, softened

75g caster sugar

170g condensed milk

4 large eggs, beaten, at room
   temperature

1 teaspoon vanilla extract

75g Gluten-Free Flour Mix A
   (see page 22)

120g frozen raspberries,
   semi-thawed

sieved icing sugar, to serve

Place a large baking tray in the oven and preheat it to 200°C/gas mark 6. Oil six individual pudding basins (approximately 150ml) and cut circles of baking parchment to line the bases.

Melt the chocolate, in a heatproof bowl, in the microwave or over a pan of simmering water – don't let the bowl touch the water – and set aside. Cream the butter and the sugar together, in a large bowl, using a hand held electric mixer, until light and fluffy. Slowly whisk in the condensed milk. Gradually beat in the eggs and the vanilla.

Stir in the melted chocolate and finally add the flour, mixing until smooth.

Divide half the chocolate mixture evenly between the pudding basins. Divide the raspberries equally between the basins. Spoon the remaining mixture evenly between the basins.

Place the moulds on the hot baking tray in the oven and cook for 12–15 minutes until puffed and risen. Remove from the oven and run a knife around the edge of the puddings to un-mould onto a serving plate. Dust with icing sugar and serve straight away.

☐ **TO STORE:** Not suitable.

✳ **TO FREEZE:** Not suitable.

STEAMED GOLDEN SYRUP SPONGE PUDDING WITH CUSTARD

A classic nursery pud, just right for a cold winter's day – soft and crumbly, with lots of syrup. The sponge will reheat perfectly on a gentle heat after being left to cool for a couple of hours.

SERVES: 4–6
PREPARATION: 15 MINUTES
COOKING: 50–55 MINUTES

For the pudding

melted butter, for greasing

3 medium eggs, at room temperature

finely grated zest of 1 lemon

120g caster sugar

4 tablespoons golden syrup

125g Gluten-Free Flour Mix A (see page 22)

½ teaspoon baking powder (see box, page 19)

1 teaspoon xanthan gum

1 teaspoon glycerine

100g vegetable oil

For the custard

600ml semi-skimmed milk

50g custard powder (see box, page 19)

caster sugar or golden syrup, to taste

Grease a 1-litre heatproof glass bowl with the butter. Place a steamer pan on the hob and half fill with water. Check the bowl will fit snugly inside the steamer container with the lid on.

In a food mixer on high speed, whisk the eggs, lemon zest and caster sugar until very thick and mousse-like.

Using a spoon warmed in hot water, place the golden syrup in the bottom of the greased bowl. Mix together the flour, baking powder and xanthan gum really well in a separate bowl. Then combine the glycerine and oil together in a jug. Remove the bowl from the food mixer and sprinkle in the flour mixture. Add the oil mixture and gently whisk it all together.

Pour the mixture into the greased glass bowl; it will be just over three-quarters full at this point. Cover tightly with buttered foil. Pop into the boiling steamer and place the lid on, then steam for 50–55 minutes. Keep an eye on the boiling water – you may need to top it up with water from the kettle.

Once cooked, the sponge will have risen almost to the top of the bowl. Carefully remove from the steamer and leave for 5 minutes to set.

Meanwhile make the custard by mixing a quarter of the milk with the custard powder in a jug. Bring the rest of the milk to the boil in a small non-stick saucepan. Once boiling, carefully pour in the cold milk and custard powder mixture, whilst gently whisking all the time. The milk should thicken straight away, and just boil. Remove from the hob and add the sugar or syrup to taste, bear in mind you will have plenty of sweetness from the pudding itself.

Remove the foil from the pudding and turn out onto a large bowl or plate. Serve straight away with plenty of hot custard.

☐ **TO STORE:** Not suitable.

✳ **TO FREEZE:** Freeze the cooled pudding in the bowl, covered with foil. Defrost for 1–2 hours. To reheat, cover with clingfilm and cook in the microwave in 30-second bursts.

SESAME SEED TOFFEE BANANAS

Bananas deep fried in a light Chinese-style batter and dipped in crisp caramel – fab! I like to toss them in the traditional coating of sesame seeds, along with some crushed brazil nuts.

SERVES: 4
PREPARATION: 20 MINUTES
COOKING: 30 MINUTES

100g Gluten-Free Flour Mix A
   (see page 22)

1½ teaspoons baking powder
   (see box, page 19)

300ml vegetable oil, for frying

4 medium bananas

2 tablespoons sesame seeds

1 tablespoon crushed, toasted
   brazil nuts (optional)

200g caster sugar

Mix the flour with the baking powder. Gradually stir 150ml cold water into the flour to make a thick, smooth paste; as a guide, it should be a little thicker than double cream and you may need to adjust the amount of water slightly, to achieve a coating batter.

Organise yourself with a couple of metal slotted spoons, kitchen paper for draining and the bowl of batter ready, so you can use it straight away.

Heat the oil in a medium, deep saucepan: it's hot enough when a cube of bread sizzles and turns golden in a few seconds.

Slice the bananas into 4 pieces each and dip a few at a time into the flour paste. Use a slotted spoon to drain the excess batter off and lift the pieces into the hot oil (a frying basket will make this easier). Deep fry the bananas in batches, for about 1½ minutes each. With a clean slotted spoon, turn them in the oil until pale golden and drain on kitchen paper. When you have cooked all the bananas, prepare the caramel.

Mix the sesame seeds with the brazil nuts, if using, and set aside. Melt the sugar with 4 tablespoons cold water in a small, heavy-based saucepan over a low heat. Stir gently, and only when all the sugar crystals are dissolved, stop stirring and allow it to boil. Bubble until the mixture turns a dark golden caramel colour – about 10 minutes. Remove from the heat.

Use two wooden skewers to pick up the banana pieces and dip them into the hot caramel sauce. Roll one side in the sesame seeds and transfer them to a sheet of baking parchment set over a wire rack. Leave the toffee bananas briefly for the caramel to harden, then serve straight away.

A note of caution: Because of the high temperatures reached by the oil and the sugar, you will need to keep a careful watch at all the stages and the pans should not be left unsupervised. I wouldn't recommend making this with children, but they will enjoy the end result!

☐ **TO STORE:** Not suitable.

✱ **TO FREEZE:** Not suitable.

CHOCOLATE MINT FONDANT CREAMS

A favourite from childhood which I've given a grown-up twist – simple, good fun and tasty.

MAKES: APPROXIMATELY 18
PREPARATION: 15 MINUTES, PLUS 1 HOUR SETTING TIME

120g condensed milk

225g icing sugar, sieved

3–4 drops natural peppermint extract

icing sugar, for dusting

25g dark chocolate (see box, page 19)

edible glitter (see box, page 19) – try www.squires-shop.com

Pour the condensed milk into a large bowl and gradually mix in the icing sugar to make a smooth paste. Next add the peppermint extract. Knead the paste until it is smooth and firm. The fondant should keep its shape; add a little more icing sugar if it seems too soft or too sticky.

Roll the fondant out, on a work surface dusted with icing sugar, to 5mm thickness and then cut into rounds with a 3cm cutter. Place the creams on baking parchment and leave in a cool place to set – this will take about 1 hour.

Melt the chocolate, in a heatproof bowl, in the microwave or over a pan of simmering water and set aside. Decorate the peppermint creams with the melted chocolate by drizzling it over in lines or dip into the melted chocolate to coat one half.

Sprinkle a little edible glitter over to give them a professional finish.

☐ **TO STORE:** Allow the chocolate to set, and store in an airtight container for up to 1 month.

✱ **TO FREEZE:** Not suitable.

SALTED CARAMEL POPCORN

I love this! Salted caramel popcorn has become all the rage over the past year or two. I find that the microwave salted variety works the best – it's easy and foolproof. If you can't get hold of microwave popcorn, this also works with regular popcorn maize.

SERVES: 2–3
PREPARATION: 5 MINUTES
COOKING: 5–15 MINUTES

100g pack salted microwave popcorn or 100g popcorn maize plus 1 tablespoon vegetable oil

100g caster sugar

25g unsalted butter

For microwave popcorn: Cook the popcorn according to the manufacturer's instructions and tip into a large bowl. Reject any hard kernels.

For popcorn maize: Heat the oil in a large pan and add the popcorn maize. Cover firmly with a lid and heat gently, shaking the pan until all the corn is popped. The trick is to listen and when the popping slows right down (after approximately 8–10 minutes), remove the pan from the heat and tip the popcorn into a large bowl.

Spread the sugar over the base of a wide, heavy-based pan, set over a medium heat, and keep an eye on it until it begins to melt and caramelise. Swirl the pan to make an even, dark golden liquid; watch carefully and take it off the heat before it gets too dark or it will taste bitter. Carefully whisk in 1 tablespoon of water and the butter and stir to a smooth, rich butterscotch.

Trickle the butterscotch onto the puffed popcorn in the bowl, using two forks to pull the clumps apart, and coat the popcorn as it cools.

☐ **TO STORE:** The popcorn will keep well in an airtight container for a couple of days.

✳ **TO FREEZE:** Not suitable.

DIRECTORY

COELIAC SOCIETIES

Your national coeliac society can provide more information about coeliac disease, put you in touch with local groups and keep you informed about events relating to coeliac disease.

UNITED KINGDOM

Coeliac UK
3rd Floor Apollo Centre
Desborough Road
High Wycombe
Buckinghamshire HP11 2QW
Tel: +44 (0)1494 474349

Coeliac UK is the national charity for people with coeliac disease and dermatitis herpetiformis. You can contact Coeliac UK via their website at www.coeliac.org.uk or by phoning their Helpline on 0845 305 2060 (Helpline open 10–4, Mon, Tue, Thu, Fri and 11–4, Wed). The Food and Drink Directory, available in print and online, lists about 10,000 products that are safe to eat.

IRELAND

The Coeliac Society of Ireland
Carmichael House
4 North Brunswick Street
Dublin 7
Tel: +353 (0)1872 1471
www.coeliac.ie

USA

Celiac Disease Foundation
13251 Ventura Blvd Ste 1
Studio City, CA 91604
Tel: +1 818 990 2354
www.celiac.org

Celiac Sprue Association
P.O. Box 31700
Omaha, NE 68131-0700
Tel: +1 402 558 0600
www.csaceliacs.org

Gluten Intolerance Group
31214 124th Ave SE
Auburn, WA 98092-3667
Tel: +1 253 833 6655
www.gluten.net

American Celiac Society Dietary Support Coalition
PO Box 23455
New Orleans, LA 70183-0455
Tel: +1 504 737 3293
www.americanceliacsociety.org

CANADA

Canadian Celiac Association
5170 Dixie Road, Suite 204
Mississauga, Ontario L4W 1E3
Tel: +1 905 507 6208
www.celiac.ca

Fondation Quebecoise de la Maladie Coeliaque
4837 rue Boyer, Bureau 230
Montreal, Quebec H2J 3E6
Tel: +1 514 529 8806
www.fqmc.org

AUSTRALIA

The Coeliac Society of Australia
Mailing Address:
PO Box 271, Wahroonga NSW 2076
Street Address:
Suite 1, 41045 Pacific Highway
Waitara NSW 2077
Tel: +61 2 9487 5177
www.coeliac.org.au

NEW ZEALAND

Coeliac Society of New Zealand
PO Box 35724, Browns Bay
North Shore City, Auckland 0753
Tel: +64 9 820 5157
www.coeliac.co.nz

SOUTH AFRICA

Coeliac Society of South Africa
PO Box 64203, Highlands North
Johannesburg 2037
Tel: +27 11 440 3431
coeliac@netactive.co.za

GLUTEN-FREE PRODUCTS

If you are unable to find gluten-free products at your local supermarket or healthfood shop, try the following online suppliers.

UNITED KINGDOM

Community Foods
Micross, Brent Terrace,
London NW2 1LT
Tel: +44 (0)208 2082966
www.communityfoods.co.uk

Doves Farm Foods
Salisbury Road, Hungerford
Berkshire, RG17 0RF
Tel: +44 (0)1488 684880
www.dovesfarm.co.uk

Glutafin
Unit 3, Rowan House
Sheldon Business Park,
Chippenham
Wiltshire, SN14 0SQ
Tel: +44 (0)800 9882470
www.glutafin.co.uk

Gluten Free Foods
Unit 270, Centennial Park
Centennial Avenue, Elstree
Borehamwood, Herts WD6 3SS
Tel: +44 (0)208 9534444
www.glutenfree-foods.co.uk

Lifestyle Health Care Ltd
Omega 250 Mamhilad
Technology Park
Pontypool NP4 0JJ
Tel: +44 (0)8452 701400
www.gfdiets.com

IRELAND

Heron Quality Foods Ltd.
Knockbrown Brandon
Co. Cork
Tel: +353 (0)233 9006
www.glutenfreedirect.com

USA

Ener-G Foods
5960 First Avenue South
PO Box 84487
Seattle, WA 98124-5787
Tel: +1 206 767 6660
www.ener-g.com

Gluten Free
www.glutenfree.com

Gluten Free Mall
www.glutenfreemall.com

Gluten Solutions
www.glutensolutions.com

Shop Organic
www.shoporganic.com

AUSTRALIA

Gluten Free Shop
553A North Road
Ormond, Victoria 3204
Tel: +61 3 9578 6400
www.glutenfreeshop.com.au

NEW ZEALAND

Gluten Free Goodies
Tel: +64 4 902 9696
www.glutenfreegoodies.co.nz

SOUTH AFRICA

Fresh Earth Food Store
103 Komatie Road,
Emmarentia, Johannesburg
Tel: +27 11 646 3470
www.freshearth.co.za

INDEX

ACKNOWLEDGEMENTS

There are so many people I would like to thank. This sort of book takes many people to help, check, re-check and publish.

Firstly, thank you to Kyle Cathie for being brave and re-signing me – hope you like it.

Thanks to Jenny Wheatley, for bringing it all together and making some sense of all the experiments; Jacqui Caulton, for the fab design; Annie Rigg and Rachel Wood, for making all the food look great; Wei Tang, spot-on as usual; Elanor Clarke and Gemma John, lovely job; and Jane Bamforth, for helping in all the areas I had forgotten about.

A big thank you to Tara Fisher for the simply wonderful photos, and for getting me to smile at the right time. Bea Harling, good friend and without whose help I don't know what I would have done when I was stuck!

Thanks to all the girls at Coeliac UK who checked and re-checked; Amy Peterson, Kathryn Miller and Jo Archer, whose help and advice has been invaluable.

To John Rush, my close friend and agent, and Luigi Bonomi – the best around by far.

Finally, Fernie – you make everything I do possible.